"Deep, elegant, and complete . . . his is a terrific book for anyone who wants to kick butt with technology. I hope my competition doesn't read it."

— Guy Kawasaki, Author of *Rules for Revolutionaries*, Chief Evangelist, Apple Computer, Inc.

"Unique in its wise employment of engaging vignettes, its affable conversational style, its remarkably wide range of topics, and its decidedly 'can-do!' air, this highly readable volume belongs in the 'must use!' section of the home library of every serious speaker, whether a nervous start-up or accomplished professional type. Having gone that route myself over recent decades, I can attest to the many valuable insights and pragmatic leads easily gleaned from this well-edited and handsomely printed volume. At once both detailed and yet also inspiring, Ringle's TechEdge *will significantly help speakers—and thereby innumerable audiences—for many years to come."*

— Professor Arthur B. Shostak, Drexel University, Professional Speaker and Futurist

"[Ringle] should be proud of your efforts. There is a great deal of valuable information that I've never come across before. [His] writing style makes the book a pleasure to read for a wide range of audiences."

— Steve Brook, Programming Chair, Select Toastmasters of Springfield, PA

*"*TechEdge *makes using technology almost as easy as reading about it."*

— Randy M. Zeitman, Philadelphia-based programmer, educator, writer, artist, and musician specializing in multimedia and the Internet.

"If, like me, you have ever been frustrated in trying to research an industry or a topic online, Bill Ringle's

TechEdge *has the simplest, most straight-forward approach to using today's technology in that arena that I have ever seen. And research is only one of the many valuable uses you will find for this book. Buy it and don't lend it out. It will be one of the best investments in your speaking career you ever made."*

— George L. Morrisey, CSP, CPAE, The Morrisey Group

"Bill Ringle, technology expert and trainer himself, explains all matters technical in clear, even eloquent, terms. He shows how to make technology enhance both the craft and the business of presenting and consulting. In a most delightful way, he demystifies the techno-babble; makes specific product recommendations; and gives very practical advice for applying high-tech whiz-bang in the real world. Geek and greenhorn alike will find this comprehensive work an invaluable guide."

— Don Blohowiak, Leadership Development Keynoter, Author of five books on leadership, change and marketing, including co-author of "The Complete Idiot's Guide to Great Customer Service"

"As speakers, trainers and consultants, we simply must keep up with the technology that helps propel our careers forward. Bill Ringle gives you the tools necessary to move to the next level and turbo charge your marketing and office. If you're serious about being a speaker, trainer or consultant, this book can help you immensely."

— Terry Brock, professional communicator, Orlando, Florida

"Bill Ringle has given everyone who speaks, trains and consults an invaluable, hands-on sourcebook of ideas, suggestions & solutions. The book blends technology discussions with applications discussions: the real TechEdge *is the creative application of technology to how we work. This book can help a whole lot."*

— Dr. Stephen J. Andriole, Chief Technology Officer, CIGNA Corporation

A word about this series from
Toastmasters International . . .

Who needs another book on public speaking, let alone a series of them? After all, this is a skill best learned by practice and "just doing it," you say.

True, but insight from people who've already been where you are might help ease some bumps along the road and provide handy advice on handling stagefright and knotty speech assignments.

After all, if practice is the best solution to public speaking excellence, why is this country so full of speakers who can't speak effectively? Consider politicians, business executives, sales professionals, teachers, and clerics who often fail to reach their audience because they make elementary mistakes, such as speaking too fast or too long, failing to prepare adequately, and forgetting to analyze their audiences.

Too often, we assume that because we try so hard to communicate, people will automatically understand us. Nothing could be further from the truth! Listeners will judge us by what they think we said, rather than what was intended or even said. Simply put, the meaning of our message—and our credibility—is determined by the reaction we get from other people. The purpose of *The Essence of Public Speaking Series,* then, is to help you in the communication process, prepare you for the unexpected, warn you of the pitfalls, and, as a result, ensure that the message you want to give is indeed the same one people hear.

This series represents the accumulated wisdom of experts in various speech-related fields. The books are written by academically trained professionals who have spent decades writing and delivering speeches, as well as training others. The series covers the spectrum of speaking scenarios: writing for the ear, using storytelling and humor, customizing particular topics for various audiences, motivating people to action, using technology for presentations, and other important topics.

Whether you are an inexperienced or seasoned public speaker, *The Essence of Public Speaking Series* belongs on your bookshelf. Because no matter how good you are, there is always room for improvement. The key to becoming a more effective speaker is in your hands: Do you have the self-discipline to put into practice the techniques and advice outlined in these books?

I honestly believe that every person who truly wants to become a confident and eloquent public speaker can become one. Success or failure in this area solely depends on attitude. There is no such thing as a "hopeless case." So, if you want to enhance your personal and professional progress, I urge you to become a better public speaker by doing two things:

■ Read these books.
■ Get on your feet and practice what you've learned.

Terrence J. McCann
Executive Director, Toastmasters International

... *and from the*
National Speakers Association

For the true professional, school is never out. *The Essence of Public Speaking Series* was developed to share ideas and information with those who desire to accelerate their development as speakers. As a community of more than 3,700 men and women dedicated to advancing the art and value of experts who speak professionally, the National Speakers Association (NSA) welcomes this comprehensive educational resource.

A broad spectrum of talented individuals make up the field of professional speaking: consultants, trainers, educators, humorists, industry specialists, authors, and many more. NSA brings this wide variety of professional speakers together to better serve their clients, advance their careers, and help them reach a higher level of personal and professional development.

Throughout *The Essence of Public Speaking Series,* you will hear the voices of NSA members offering their expertise and experiences. This sharing of ideas and knowledge is a key element of NSA membership. NSA's founder and Chairperson Emeritus Cavett Robert said, "Experience is the only thing that's worth more secondhand than first-hand. We don't live long enough to learn through trial and error, so it's best to get your O.P.E. degree—Other People's Experience."

The "information age" is creating a huge demand for professional speakers. The fact that education is one of the top growth industries in the world should come as no surprise. What may seem surprising, however, is the fact that when we're speaking of education, we are not referring to the traditional colleges and universities. Instead, it is the learning that is conducted daily in the hotels and corporate training facilities. The "faculty" for these learning experiences are often professional speakers.

Speakers are a key element in the growing meetings business. The American Society of Association Executives reports that the meeting market is a $75 billion industry. Moreover, the American Society for Training and Development estimates that well over $100 billion is expended annually in the field of human resource development alone.

The audiences of the new millennium will be different from the audiences of the past. They are not content to sit and be passive listeners; they want to take an active role in their own learning; and require cutting-edge information presented in a technologically savvy manner. The speakers and trainers who fail to deliver the information and content these audiences can utilize immediately will notice that audiences are not afraid to vote with their feet.

So, we welcome you to the world of speaking. As you read the volumes in this series, you will explore many facets of public and professional speaking. You are about to embark on an important learning experience—one that will broaden your vision as a public speaker and perhaps instill a desire to make speaking an important dimension of your career. NSA, the "Voice of the Speaking Profession," stands ready to provide you with information on the speaking industry and the resources you need to make a speaking career a viable option.

Edward E. Scannell, CSP, CMP
Interim Executive Vice President
National Speakers Association

TechEdge

Using Computers to Present and Persuade

WILLIAM J. RINGLE

WILLIAM D. THOMPSON
Series Editor

ALLYN AND BACON

Boston   London   Toronto   Sydney   Tokyo   Singapore

Trademark Credits continue on page 180,
which constitutes a continuation of this copyright page

For Sue, my life partner,
whose love, encouragement, support,
and patience allow me to
explore new frontiers and
share what I've learned to
help others become
more productive and confident
in this increasingly
technical and complicated world.

And for Nicholas, our son,
who brings such simple delight and joy
into our lives.

Contents

List of Illustrations

Introduction

Welcome to *TechEdge*, the book that explains how to use technology to enhance your speaking, training, and consulting. When presenting to a group is critical to your work, you can use technology to achieve your audience's goals and increase your value.

Whether you speak in front of groups frequently or seldom, under formal or informal circumstances, this book will show you how to embrace technology appropriately to enhance your preparation, development, and delivery.

WHY YOU NEED THIS BOOK

Jim Barber, past president of the Florida Speakers Association, was delivering a talk on finances to chapter leaders of the National Speakers Association when he said, "You've got to use a budget to project your cash flow. It's really easy. It will take you half an hour if you sit down with pencil and paper—an hour if you use a computer." Along with the rest of the chapter leaders, I smiled and chuckled. Jim had demonstrated in a single sentence the necessity and frustration of using computers.

It is no different in the speaking profession than in other business areas—everyone can identify with the sentiment. In that meeting, everyone was somewhere along the road to mastering technology in their business and either had or will face the inevitable snags, glitches, and hiccups along the way.

I wrote this book with the intention of reducing the number (and severity) of the bumps along the road of using technology as a presenter. I will accomplish this in four ways:

xvi   Introduction

1. By giving you information to help familiarize you with
    the different technology areas.
2. By explaining the issues and giving real-world examples
    so you can make well-informed decisions about how to
    acquire and use technology.
3. By sharing how professional presenters and consultants
    are using technology and how it is serving their needs.
4. By making recommendations on action steps. Experience is
    the best teacher, so I will offer you guided instructions as
    well as challenging exercises to help develop your skills and
    understanding through interactions with the technology.

WHAT YOU CAN EXPECT FROM THIS BOOK

You should be aware of three features you will not find in this
book that are too common in books on how busy people use
technology.

First, this book is not about how much the author knows
but about how much you can learn. I want you to know more
about and do more with technology. I will explain clearly the
capabilities and uses of technology as well as the steps to take
to continue exploring and learning on your own.

Second, this book is not an information dump. Instead of
giving you a 400-page tome full of raw data, I would rather
explain specific ideas and provide guidelines for using technology well. In *TechEdge,* you won't find web site listings
unless I explain why it would be worth your time to visit
them; you won't find 30 pages about HTML specifications
(the code underlying web page design). My intention is that
you find *TechEdge* a refreshing alternative to general computer
or Internet books.

Third, this book is not for computer experts or computer
expert wannabes. It's for the business presenter or consultant
and students of all ages and backgrounds who want to learn
more about how to use technology to gain an edge in their

work. Business moves too rapidly today to spend time on professional development and not get a return on the investment. In *TechEdge,* you will find succinct, practical information, strategies, resources, and advice focused on the professional who wants to learn more about technology to achieve better results.

CONVENTIONS USED

Because I have oriented this book so as to help you achieve better results, I have included some instructions for you to carry out with a computer. Remember the following:

- You should be familiar with the following operations: pointing the mouse, clicking objects, double-clicking objects, selecting and dragging objects, pulling down menu bar items, and popping up and selecting menu items. These are fundamental computer skills, but you should refer to your computer operations manuals if you have questions about them.
- Characters that you are meant to type are set in a monospaced font. For instance, if you are instructed to type "subscribe" into the body of the e-mail message, you would type the word but not the quotation marks in the designated place.
- Though a web or e-mail address might be too long to fit on a single line when printed in this book, note that neither web addresses nor e-mail addresses contain spaces or return characters.
- I have put web addresses in parentheses and bold type. Online, the convention is to use angle brackets and the full Internet address, including the service prefix, but in print, this looks less friendly than the parenthesis convention. The web addresses you will encounter in this book typically will not include the full service name but will include the full path name. For example, when you encounter a description of the TechEdge web site

(**techedge.BillRingle.com**), you will see the web address; when you actually enter this information into your web browser, you will need to remember to type the full address, "`http://techedge.BillRingle.com`", in order to access the web site.

BEFORE YOU BEGIN

The information and suggestions in this book are for educational purposes only. Do not take any statements made as unqualified recommendations for your business. Smart consultants and other businesspeople realize that you need good ideas (which this book supplies) *and* good implementation (which you supply). You alone know best what steps you and your business are ready for. Know the terrain, experiment, and adapt as you get smarter and more experienced.

High technology moves faster than any other business segment, and the Internet in particular is an unpredictable, rapidly changing field. If you plotted human years, dog years, and Internet years as three lines on a chart, you could see that each category has a rate of change seven times greater than the previous category. Nimble businesses can turn an industry inside out virtually overnight. Decisions about which technology users have no information affect them profoundly. For example, some of the web sites pointed out in *TechEdge* may have moved since publication and not left forwarding addresses. Some may have closed down permanently. Some may be giving better or worse information than they were when I researched them. While I've made every attempt to recommend reliable online resources, you should be aware of the mercurial nature of online information publishing.

To realize the greatest value from it, use this book in two ways. First, let this book help introduce you to the intersection between the world of technology and the business of speaking, training, and consulting. Both are fascinating places, and with a helpful, guided tour, you can cut months, if not years, off your learning curve. Second, let this book help you ask the right questions of people and interpret the responses you get. You will be the final decision maker. After all, you know your situation and will be able to evaluate the ways you spend your money and your time.

This book explores the technical edge of enhancing your business: How to find your tech edge, how to sharpen it, and how to chart your course for continuous learning.

Acknowledgments

I'd like to thank my friends and co-workers at StarComm Development, Inc. for their efforts in helping to make this book a reality. Peg Moody reviewed early drafts of *TechEdge*. Peggy Ryan McGroarty provided organizational support throughout the project. I gratefully acknowledge Rob Ditto for his excellent technical editing and supplemental research.

Bill Thompson had a vision for a series of books that would represent the cutting-edge knowledge and practice for speakers, trainers, and consultants. I am honored to have been asked to write this book on technology as part of *The Essence of Public Speaking Series*.

Through luck, grace, and perseverence, I've been fortunate to have the opportunity to present to people around the world—from Teterboro, New Jersey, to Tokyo, Japan. I appreciate what I've learned from the individuals who have attended my presentations and trainings. Your insights and contributions are invaluable, and I look forward to continuing to learn from and present to audiences near and far.

I'd also like to acknowledge my personal mentors and professional colleagues whose contributions have helped shape my life and my perspectives. Thanks for your provocative questions, your inspiring examples, your humor, your challenges, your friendship, and your enduring influence: Joyce Garvin, Nancy Kline, Charlie Kreiner, Tony Robbins, Michael Young, Ken Blackney, Glenna Salsbury, Corrine Dapice, Fred Bockmann, Marjorie Brody, Don Blohowiak, Guy Kawasaki, and Richard Zarro.

Technology Is More Than Computers

Those of us who communicate for a living realize that technology is simply a means to amplify the message we are delivering.

Bill Ringle

TELEPHONES

Jack's management training company, operated from a spare bedroom in his home, has grown successfully during its first two years. However, his phone service is a mess. Clients on the West Coast call during dinner. Faxes attempt to connect to his personal computer in the middle of the night. Messages taken by his teenage children are often indecipherable. Jack needs to apply his management skills to untangling his phone communications.

Working from home blurs the line between your personal and business life enough. The last thing you need is the stress of not knowing how to answer an incoming call. While a businesslike greeting on your answering machine might make your mother-in-law snicker, an informal greeting from your teenager jeopardizes your credibility with clients.

A simple solution calls for the addition of a distinctive ring pattern to your existing phone line. Many local phone companies offer this service. What it means is that your current phone line will be assigned a second phone number. When people call this second number, your phone will ring with a different sound. The advantages: you save the cost of an additional phone-line installation; the monthly fee for a distinctive ring pattern is less than the cost of a second line; the ring sounds like a normal ring pattern to the caller; and if you decide to get a separate line at some later date, you can transfer this number to that new line. However, your local phone service may not offer distinctive ring patterns in your calling area. In that case, you will have to spend a few more dollars and get a second line installed.

Getting a second line makes sense when you need to be speaking on the business line while other members of the family are using the home line. You also might want to add special options for the business line, such as call waiting, call forwarding, caller ID, and so on. Besides, having a separate phone for your business makes writing off calls as a tax deduction much simpler.

While the service person is boring a hole through the outside wall of your home to install a business line, you might as well take advantage of the situation and have a fax line installed as well. Although you can use your computer for outgoing faxes that don't require your signature, you should invest $300 to $500 for a simple plain-paper fax machine for incoming faxes. (Be sure to get a *plain-paper* machine—faxes printed on the more common thermal paper can be irritating to deal with, particularly when you need to sign the fax and then refax the signed document.) While putting coins in a parking meter has been heralded as giving the best return of peace of mind per dollar invested, having a dedicated fax machine would make the top-ten list in this department! If you've lost one important fax because you forgot to leave your computer or modem powered on, you've lost one too many. In addition, you want to do all you can to represent to the outside world that you have a reliable communications system.

When you are not at your desk to answer an incoming call, have either an answering machine, voice mail service from your phone company, or answering service take your messages. Picking one over the others is a matter of taste, style, and your need for flexibility. The quality of service you get with a hired firm can vary from hour to hour and week to week if the business has multiple operators. A cheap answering machine sounds like a cheap answering machine and projects a certain image for your business. And voice mail may seem like "voice mail jail" to your callers if the provided menus and options are difficult to use. Consider some of the issues outlined in Table 1.1 on page 4.

One last issue to consider concerning telephones is that of hands-free devices. Speaker phones and headsets top the list of technologies used to accomplish this objective. Many phones now come with speaker capability, which means that the caller's voice is projected from a speaker and your voice is transmitted via a built-in microphone—holding the handset is unnecessary. The prime advantages are that your hands are free to write, type, or hold materials and that you can have other people in the room with you participate in the call. The downside of a speaker phone is that your voice quality may be degraded or distorted by poor equipment. Your voice will typically sound farther away. If you are asked more than once whether you are "calling from the moon," you should move closer to the phone when using the speaker option. You should also look at the possibility of upgrading your telephone to a more sophisticated system.

Table 1.1

Telephone Answering Solutions

Answering Machine	Answering Service
■ One-time investment	■ Ongoing cost
■ Your own voice used to greet	■ Another voice used—may be better/worse than your voice
■ Consistent message	
■ Answers 24 hours a day	■ Greeting may vary with operator
■ Can retrieve messages remotely	■ May only operate during business hours
	■ Can dictate, fax, or e-mail messages

Phone Company Voice Mail

■ Ongoing cost (should be less than dedicated answering service)

■ Your voice used to greet

■ Consistent message

■ Answers 24 hours a day

■ Able to retrieve messages remotely

■ Resistant to power failures at your home or office (though not to phone-company equipment failures)

■ Can be set up to page you when messages arrive or deliver messages to another phone number

A headset is like a speaker phone you wear. The speaker piece covers one or both ears and the microphone is held within an inch or two of your mouth. Some headsets connect to a base unit via a wire; others free you to walk around because they transmit signals between the phone and the headset.

MICROPHONES

Fred needed to address several dozen businesspeople he
had never met before at a workshop, and he was nervous about it. A friend of his who belonged to the local
Toastmasters group asked him if he was planning to use
a microphone. This idea had never occurred to Fred. His
friend explained, "Sure, when you're nervous, your
muscles contract, including the ones in your throat
you'll be counting on to produce your voice. Speaking
in front of a group of strangers is one of the three
biggest fears for adults. Using a microphone will take
some of the pressure off you because knowing that
everyone can hear you will be one less thing to worry
about. This way, you can focus more of your attention
on the content of your talk."

You have probably used microphones in the past. However, it
is valuable to know a bit about the technical capabilities and
intended applications of different types of microphones.

A unidirectional microphone, one which picks up input
from a single direction, is often attached to a podium. Your
voice will sound best when your mouth is between four and
eight inches from the head, or top part, of the microphone.
Some of these microphones have a gooseneck that allows you
to grasp the neck and twist it to accommodate a particular
angle (it makes for better rapport with the audience as well as
for better photographs when the microphone or gooseneck is
not blocking your face).

As you become more confident and develop your style as
a platform speaker, you will likely be coming out from
behind the lectern. Sometimes, the podium microphone can
unclip from its attachment and be carried if the length of the
cord permits. Other times, a separate wireless microphone is

used. High-end, hand-held microphones contain a micro-transmitter that eliminates having to manage a long cord as you move from one part of the stage to another.

Lavaliere microphones give you even more freedom because they are smaller, lighter, and free up your hands as well as avoid the cord problems. Lavaliere mikes can be worn on the lapel of your jacket, around your neck, or clipped to the collar of your shirt or blouse. When clipped on, the microphone is usually positioned near the second shirt button, about two inches down from your collar.

The basic lavaliere unit looks like a black or grey foam ball, the size of a walnut or smaller. The foam covering over the microphone is called a windscreen, and it helps reduce breathing sounds and the rustle of clothing. A thin wire cable three feet long connects the microphone to a radio transmitter. The cable usually runs under a speaker's shirt and around to the back where the radio transmitter is clipped to the back of a belt. For less formal presentations, it is perfectly acceptable to be more casual about hiding the cable.

Headsets, which combine a microphone with earphones, are sometimes used for trade-show floor presentations. If you've seen ads for the long-distance companies, you've seen actors and actresses wearing these devices when the announcer says, "And operators are standing by!" Like headphones, headsets are held in place by a band of metal (usually coated with plastic) riding around the top or back of your head and anchored with pads on either side of your head, near your ears. The band is adjustable, so one size can be made to fit nearly any head size. On one side, typically the left, a plastic arm comes down from the anchor point to position a microphone within an inch of your mouth. Again, a fuzzy ball should cover this microphone to smooth out the sound of your voice.

These headsets can be wired or wireless, depending on their cost. If you present with a wired headset, be especially careful to manage the cable with one free hand when you move or you can hurt yourself when the headset gets pulled away from you.

Surface-mount microphones are used in group situations. Rather than unidirectional, they are omnidirectional, featuring equal sensitivity in all directions. These microphones are useful for small-group conference calls and for recording the activities during a seminar at which participant feedback is recorded without a microphone being passed from one speaker to another.

Of course, microphones themselves are only input devices. They convert your voice into an electrical signal which is fed into an amplifier, which then projects your voice through a speaker system. Microphones typically have an on-off switch; some wireless microphones have a standby switch to prevent feedback squawking through the amplifiers.

Another measurement of a microphone's capabilities is its frequency response. This refers to the range of sound that the microphone picks up. A frequency range of 50 to 20,000 Hz (hertz) is greater than one of 100 to 14,000 Hz, and you should expect to pay more for a more sensitive microphone. The wider the frequency range, the better the audio will sound when it is amplified or recorded.

When you plan to speak into a microphone during a talk, you open up a world of interesting possibilities. Once you have the microphone and amplifier system wired, you can mix in music. You can record your speech and use it as a demonstration tape. You can digitize the recording and play it over the Internet for potential clients. The possibilities are unlimited and the benefits enormous, especially considering the short time needed to become familiar with the technology of microphones.

35 MM PROJECTORS

Mark agreed to give a talk at the local Chamber of Commerce on the engineering aspects of Egyptian architecture. He could combine what he knew as a civil engineer with the photos he had taken during his vacation a few months before. It was an exciting opportunity to share some good information, but he was puzzled about how to present the information. Holding up the four-by-six-inch pictures wouldn't allow even the front row to see them clearly. Passing them around would lose the connection between the building and the point he was trying to make. Should he make up posters? That would be good for a display after the talk but not effective during the presentation.

Luckily, Mark's neighbor Emil ran the A/V department of the high school and offered to help. Emil suggested, "Mark, as long as you still have the negatives from your vacation pictures, you can take them down to the local camera shop and have them produce 35 mm slides. I'll be happy to bring over a 35 mm projector and help you learn how to operate it. In less than an hour, you can learn to set up your slides in the tray and the ins and outs of using the projector. On the night of your presentation, you can take the projector over to the Chamber of Commerce hall. I've even got a screen if you need it. Just remember, I've got to have the equipment back in time for school in the morning!"

35 mm projectors display clear, bright images in a darkened room. These projectors are great for showing picture slides. For the past three decades, they have assisted both educators and businesspeople alike in conveying visual information to groups.

Modern projector units use a circular slide tray that typically holds 80 to 120 slides. When a command is sent to advance a slide, a motor moves the slide tray forward one position so a slide can drop down in front of the projector lamp and be displayed on the screen. Older-model projectors held 20 slides and required the operator to advance the slides manually because electricity was used only to light the projector bulb. The advantage of the 35 mm projectors is that the control unit can simplify operations considerably. From a hand-held control device, you can move slides ahead, back up to show a previous slide, turn the lamp on or off, and even focus the lens (which is an important capability when not all of your pictures were taken at the same focus range).

Whether you are presenting to a class of 20 or to a conference of 2,000, a slide projector is highly versatile and can project a sharp, clear, color image for an economical investment in both start-up equipment and ongoing production materials. Each roll of film converted to 35 mm slides costs less than $10.

The downside of 35 mm slides is that they are bulky to carry around in the tray. As anyone who has used them in various places can tell you, it is a nightmare if an unsecured tray gets tipped over because all the slides have to be put back in order and placed face-forward, right-side-up in the slide tray once again. Marking the cardboard surrounding each slide in pencil simplifies this process but is laborious and creates an inflexible system. In addition, a room needs to be quite dark in order to get the best results with a 35 mm projector, thus limiting your ability to interact with the audience.

Perhaps the greatest limitation of 35 mm slides is their inflexibility. If your presentation is not one that can be sustained by photograph after photograph, you will want to project words on the screen, using a text of your talking points. Without a computer, this is a very difficult or expensive proposition. With a computer, you can easily generate the text and print it to a slide format. Some professional presenters have become highly expert and very enthusiastic about using slides. However, once you have a computer, you may bypass the slide projector altogether and mix photographic slides on the spur of a moment with materials like a text outline of your talking points, charts, maps, and other graphics. In addition, when slides are presented on a computer rather than by slide projector, it is a simple matter to add music, recorded speech, and movies to create a more compelling presentation for your audience.

OVERHEAD PROJECTORS

When Nora's supervisor encouraged her to apply as a presenter at the hospital's in-service workshop, she never thought she'd be selected. Now, holding the workshop announcement in her hand and reading her program title and her name on the brochure made it seem all too real. All the good ideas she had wanted to share about proper nutrition slipped from her mind as she realized that the workshop was only four weeks away. Fortunately, she had created an outline of her proposal and could work from that starting point. But she was very nervous about speaking in front of dozens of her co-workers at the end of the month.

"You've got to believe you're going to blow them away, Nora," her sister Cathy encouraged her. Cathy's experience as a corporate trainer was finally allowing her to help out her older sister. "Listen, I'll help you make up your transparencies to help keep you on track—you've got a ton of material to work from. When the audience is looking up at the screen, they're not looking at you. You can take that time to take a deep breath and gather what you are going to say. It'll be a cinch. You've been in that hospital for 6 years and you've got almost 14 years as a dietitian. You're going to do great!"

Overhead projectors are by far the most common way to project text and pictures on a screen to share with an audience.

They are also one of the easiest tools to learn how to use. You would recognize the table-top box shape with the glass top and crooked neck anywhere. In 10 seconds, you can be trained to flip the power switch on and to place your transparencies on the glass top so the projector can send light up and through them to a reflective mirror head that is used to position and focus the image on a screen. It might take two or three minutes to master moving the knob on the head for focusing. Accomplished overhead presenters remember to make sure that every single transparency they put on the overhead is lined up so it projects a level image onto the screen.

These projectors weigh 20 pounds or more, so although some of the newer ones fold down into a handy carrying suitcase, they are not easy to lug around. In addition, the glass plate, the mirror head, and bulbs are fragile and can break in transit if not treated carefully.

Transparencies, sometimes also called slides or foils, can hold text, display colors, and even show photographs. To make a transparency, you can bring any printed material to a copy shop, which will run them through a photocopier. Instead of a copy on paper, however, you get a copy on a thin film of acetate that you put on the glass of the overhead projector. If you have a laser printer and want to print transparencies on your own, you can buy a box of blank acetate sheets at an office supply store. Be very careful that you have the right kind of acetate before sending a sheet through your printer, because the wrong brand could melt inside the laser writer and generate a costly repair bill.

Some presenters are very skilled at using transparencies during a talk and revealing certain portions of a list one point at a time to increase audience interest. Another way to produce more interactivity with a group is to write on a transparency with a colored marking pen. The marking pens should be water soluble so you can wipe the transparency off afterward.

The greatest problem with a set of transparencies is having them stick together due either to static electricity or to
having the toner on the front of one slide rub off on the back
of a previous slide. Putting a sheet of white paper between all
your slides overcomes both these problems. The stack of
slides with interleaved paper can fit snugly into an empty
transparency box.

If you are fanatical about neatness and order (or you just
value your time), you can take each slide out of the box,
show it on screen, replace it face down in the cover of the
transparency box along with the in-between paper, and then
place the next slide on the overhead. It's a neat system for
keeping your slides in good shape.

If you develop a presentation that will be used several
times, you might want to investigate two methods for pre-
serving your slides. First, you can insert your slides in plastic
page covers. The plastic page covers can then be inserted into
a three-ring binder. If you present with the slides in the covers, be sure to use an overhead with an extra-high intensity
lamp because the additional plastic dims the projected bright-
ness of the slide.

In addition, check out cardboard mounting frames for
overhead slides. Bound on three sides, open on one, these
frames contain a slit for you to slip a transparency into. A
complementary receptacle that fits over the top of the overhead projector helps you place your framed overheads neatly
and evenly.

TECH TIP *A motto of the good presenter is "Have Something to
Say and Say It Well." The motto of the experienced
presenter is "Always Have a Backup Plan for Delivering Your
Presentation." The greatest vulnerability for users of overhead
projectors is the possibility of the bulb burning out in the mid-*

dle of a talk. Higher-end overhead projectors have a built-in remedy to this problem, which is to have two bulbs installed. If bulb A blows out, turn off the power, switch to bulb B, then switch on the power once more. If the projector you are using does not have this feature, be sure to arrive early enough to get a spare bulb from a technician and learn how to install it. Of course, if you own the projector, bring your own spare and know how to use it.

AUDIO AND VIDEO

Dianne had just hung up the phone after talking with the speaker's bureau. She sighed. Another presentation date lost because a meeting planner wasn't confident enough to book her without having heard her present. Meeting planners who had heard Dianne were eager to work with her. Dianne needed a demo tape to send out to potential clients and agents, but she didn't know how to start. She got on her computer and sent an e-mail message to one of her National Speakers Association (NSA) friends who lived across the country. Dianne asked how to go about getting material for a demo tape—should she do it live or in a studio? What did she need and where could she get the equipment?

The next day, Dianne's friend wrote back saying that all Dianne needed to do was to start gathering recordings of her live presentations. Before too long, she could bring the raw material to a recording studio and have them put together a professional demo tape with a studio introduction, set-up music, transition messages, and all the other professional touches. Dianne's friend concluded her e-mail response, "It's become too competitive in the marketplace today, Dianne. In the old days, we could just click on a pocket recorder during a talk and send that in as a demo tape. Those days are gone. Good luck with your tape—see you at the national convention in July!"

Recording yourself with a pocket recorder is a great way to review your presentations for self-evaluation. Pick up a $50 recorder at an electronics store. However, when it comes to recording your presentations to play for others, take some extra care with the quality of the recording. After all, any noise, feedback, dropout, or distortions in sound will reflect on your business.

For presenters who do not want to invest in the necessary hardware and time to learn to use it well, the route to take is partnering. When you present at a conference or workshop, ask in advance if your work is going to be recorded. If it is, ask if you can have the master tape after the conference sponsor is done with it. If there are no plans to record, you might look into renting recording equipment.

If you own your own wireless microphone amplifier system, you will need a quality tape recorder to jack into the signal receiver. A high-end Sony, Aiwa, Panasonic, or Nakamichi tape deck will do nicely. Some speakers today are finding the convenience and fidelity differences of digital audio tape recorders to be worth the added expense.

SUMMARY

As a speaker, trainer, or consultant, you should get acquainted with basic speakers' technology before you buy a computer. In Chapter 1, you learned about several types of technology that will be useful to you.

- Telephone service options, such as separate home, business, and fax lines; caller ID; distinctive ringing options; and voice mail services
- Telephone equipment options, such as separate fax machines, answering machines, and headsets
- Different microphones that will allow your audience to hear you and you to present comfortably

- Slide projectors and overhead projectors, the basic tools for presenting visual aids to your audience
- Advanced audio-visual equipment possibilities, such as tape recorders and digital audio tape recorders, which can help you with self-evaluation and preparing demos

 Just as good writers are good readers, good speakers are always paying attention to good speeches. At the next speech you hear, take note of the technology used to support the presentation.

Computer
Technology 101

This chapter explains what computer systems are, how they are used, and what details you should be familiar with as a speaker, trainer, or consultant.

MAKING SENSE OF COMPUTER LINGO

Johnny, who lives close to Chicago's O'Hare Airport, had given an open invitation to his road warrior buddies: if they were in town to speak or to meet with a client, they should look him up and drop by. Bob had known Johnny for years, so when he booked a Saturday seminar in the Windy City, he decided to stay overnight at his friend's house. In the morning, Johnny stood at the living room window, eating a bowl of cereal. Bob gulped down hot coffee in between bites of Danish while riffling through the Sunday paper.

"Hey, Bob, I heard you got a new laptop. What did you get?"

"The new ThinkPad, of course. 150 MHz, 1.2 GB hard drive, full-screen, active matrix display, CD-ROM built in—the works. Set me back a few bucks, but it's worth it as a travel machine. I've got my whole office in the palms of my hands. How about yourself, Johnny?"

"Oh, I'm happy with the PowerBook 3400 I bought earlier this year. It's got a crystal-clear display of 500 by 600, 240 MHz Power PC Chip, and a drive bay that I can load with either a CD-ROM or a floppy drive.

When I'm back at the office, I can synchronize the laptop with my scheduling server and send my staff messages on our local network. Come on back and let me show you. We've gotten a lot of new equipment since the last time you visited."

OK, time out. I recognize that this book is being read by professionals and colleagues who probably don't spend half their waking hours reading technical magazines and participating in techie online discussions. If your eyes just glazed over, go splash some cold water on your face, then come back and we'll go over the technospeak step by step so you will gain a better understanding of what these two guys were babbling about.

Computers today come in three basic sizes: desktop, tower, and laptop. Desktop machines are meant to be placed on the desk and generally have a monitor sitting on top. When a repair or upgrade is required, the lid of a desktop unit can be lifted off to expose the circuit boards, slots, and RAM bays. Tower computers stand upright and can be placed on an office floor or a desktop. If put on a floor, they must be protected against water damage caused by dampness or territorial pets—especially dogs (an actual risk for home-office workers). Laptop computers (also known as notebook computers) truly are portable, even though their performance is comparable to desktop machines.

Keep the following points in mind about these different types of computer:

■ Desktops and tower machines are usually more powerful than laptops but not because of their size alone. The processor and the speed rating determine a computer's power.

■ The major advantage of a tower is expandability. With its additional size come drive bays into which an additional hard drive, a Zip drive, a CD-ROM player, or another peripheral can be added.

■ Computers are called servers when they are dedicated to file sharing or specific Internet activities such as being a mail host or web site.

■ The terms *microcomputer, desktop computer, tower system, workstation,* and *PC* refer to roughly the same class of computers. The press, trade magazines, industry analysts, and general public have misused these terms so badly that we are best aided by Blackney's Rule, which states that you know the type of computer you're using by the number of friends needed to move it. A small child can carry a laptop computer. The average adult has no trouble moving a microcomputer. A minicomputer requires two to four people working together to lift it. Mainframes require at least as many people to move as a Volkswagen, often more. (This rule comes from Ken Blackney, computer consultant and developer of the NavEx utility.)

MONITORS

Monitors display the video output of a computer. Picture elements, called pixels, receive a signal which tells each element to display a particular color, usually red, green, or blue (referred to as an RGB display). To understand better the production of a color picture, imagine standing in a museum looking at a portrait of Benjamin Franklin. It's a large portrait, so you are standing a good distance away for better viewing. You walk closer, and as you do, you notice that the picture is made up of colored balls—gumballs, in fact! The Franklin Institute Science Museum in Philadelphia hosted a display of its namesake, Ben Franklin, in just this fashion. This display showed how pixels create a picture. In the portrait, each dot was a gumball of a different color. Likewise, on your monitor, each pixel lights up with a specified color.

The nonedible, computer monitors you should be looking at have the following features:

■ **Size:** You measure monitors by diagonal width of the screen. Typical monitors have either 15-inch or 17-inch screens for desktop/tower units. Laptops have 10-inch or 12-inch screens but can usually display the same number of pixels on screen, just more tightly packed together.

■ **Resolution:** Resolution refers to the sharpness and clarity of an image whether displayed on screen or on paper. IBM developed a video display standard for personal computers called VGA (video graphics array). VGA monitors support a resolution of 640 by 480, but only 16 colors are available. The eye can discern millions of colors, so this standard was superseded by SVGA (Super VGA), which provides support for up to 16 million colors, depending on the size of the video random access memory (also known as VRAM) available on the computer. The more VRAM, the more colors a monitor can display. SVGA monitors can display resolutions of 800 by 600, 1024 by 768, 1280 by 1024, and 1600 by 1200. The most common configurations are 800 by 600 and 1024 by 768. Graphic artists, newsletter editors, and others who need to see two full pages of text and graphics side by side opt for 21-inch monitors and the denser resolution displays.

Multiscan monitors can be configured via software to switch between two or more resolutions, which is advantageous when you need to view how someone on a different resolution would see a display or when you want to squeeze more screen into the display area of your monitor.

Here are some other important monitor facts and recommendations.

■ In advertisements, monitors are sometimes shown on top of the computer. That may be all right for some monitors and some computers. Do not put a large monitor on top of a computer case that is made of plastic or the case may

crack. Monitors with 17-inch screens or larger should not
be put on any other piece of equipment, just the top of
your desk. These monitors are very large and very heavy.

■ Check to make sure your laptop computer has a video-out
port, which can be connected to a projector. Projectors
can range from large color television screens to LCD pan-
els that sit atop overhead projectors to true video projectors. That video out port is a key feature requirement if
you plan to use your laptop for making presentations.

■ Video RAM (VRAM) differs from regular RAM. VRAM is
used to store information about the picture rather than to
run applications. Typically, computers have 512 KB or 1
MB of VRAM. The more VRAM your cpu (or its video
card) has, the greater the pixel density your monitor can
display and therefore the more colors it can render.

STORAGE DEVICES

The first category of storage devices most people think of are
disk drives. Disk drives are devices that read and write data to
a disk. A floppy disk drive works with a floppy disk, which is
usually encased in a hard plastic case for easier handling and
better protection. Traditional floppy disks are relatively low
capacity storage devices, holding 770 KB in their low density
variety and 1.44 MB in their high density variety. Hard disk
drives write to and read from a rigid disk platter which spins
inside a protected metal enclosure. Hard disks hold much
more data, from a few hundred KB to several GB. Both floppy
drives and hard disk drives can be used internally or externally
with computers. New computers typically come with an internal floppy drive and a 2 GB or larger internal hard drive.

Some new computers come with a factory-installed high-
capacity floppy disk drive that stores 100 MB on a single cartridge. The best known among this class of drives is the Zip
Drive, manufactured by Iomega Corporation. Zip disks are

excellent devices for moving or storing large amounts of data that can be modified at a later date.

Most computers today also come with a CD-ROM (compact disk-read only memory) drive as standard equipment. CD-ROMs read CDs. They don't write to CDs. The fact that CDs cannot be written to (accidentally or purposely) in a CD-ROM drive makes this an ideal medium for such purposes as program installers, clip art collections, and data archives. The CD-ROM rating of 2X, 4X, and 8X refers to the speed at which the drive reads data; faster speeds are significant only when you are running applications or reading data from a CD, which is less common than using a CD for an installation disk.

CD-ROM drives are slower than hard drives. While hard drives can access data in 9 to 30 milliseconds (ms), CD-ROMs take between 100 and 800 ms to access data.

PRINTERS

In the early days of the personal computer, printers were noisy and the results were not very impressive. In an effort to combat the noise, some offices purchased large plexiglass and foam enclosure hoods for their dot matrix printers which muffled the noise considerably. Early printer technology was based on a letter head striking paper through a ribbon. If you were looking for a hot tip for computer printers in 1985, you would be thrilled to know about electric-powered ribbon re-inking devices!

Thermal transfer printers were an attempt at lowering the cost and increasing the quality of the print output. Rather than use an impact technology, a waxy ink substance was heated and transferred to the paper through micro-pinholes at the time of printing. These devices produced attractive output, especially the later ones that could print different colors, but they were slow and prone to clogs in the ink holes.

When the first laser writers came out in 1986, along with them came a revolutionary technology for creating a match between what you created on the screen and what was printed on paper. Adobe introduced a page layout description language called Postscript, low-level instructions that the computer communicated to the printer. Postscript has evolved over the years and is still the industry-standard pace-setter for high-quality printers and other imaging devices.

Today, you can select from much more sophisticated printers that are much smaller, of much better quality, and also much more affordable. Just remember:

- The quality of a printer is determined by several factors. Look at the dots per inch (dpi) and special enhancement technologies. A few years ago, 300 dpi was standard. Now 600 dpi printers have raised the bar. Industrial strength printers, such as those you will find at copy shops and publishing houses, start at 1200 dpi print resolution. If you are buying a printer today for your business, you are strongly urged to consider the 600 dpi class of laser printers.

- Some ink-jet printers produce 300 dpi; some produce 600 dpi; and some take the middle road of 300 × 600 dpi. This third category gives you much better-looking output than the 300 dpi for less cost than a 600 dpi printer.

- Printer enhancement technologies such as Hewlett Packard's PCL (printer control language) and Apple Computer's FinePrint produce partial dots around the edges of a letter to make the curves smoother and straight edges crisper. This technology is quite effective on 300 dpi but offers hardly any benefit when printing at 600 dpi and above.

- The differences for text in print quality between different printers of the same resolution category are less significant than the differences for graphics. Horizontal or vertical banding can occur when the toner is not evenly distributed; black areas may not output as uniformly black for the same reason. The best way to evaluate printers is to compare output from a file of your own materials printed out on different printers. Computer stores and convention shows provide opportunities for this type of comparison shopping, but ask for the sales representative's help only when you are actually interested in making a printer purchase.

■ The two steps you can take to have the greatest control over the quality of your output once you have a printer are: (1) Use a high-quality paper designed for laser printers. This paper is more expensive, so it might not be used for everyday output. However, for special letters, brochures, or proposals, this paper has a greater opacity and higher reflectivity, which produces brighter, cleaner, sharper output, especially with graphics. (2) Adjust the level of toner dispensed. Many printers allow you to increase or decrease the amount of toner used to produce the marks on paper, whether they are marks that look like letters, lines, logos, or anything else. If set to a low level, your output looks grey instead of black; set too high and your output looks smudged and muddy. Check to see if your printer offers this capability and experiment to make sure you are getting the best results from your equipment for your needs.

■ Stock up on a spare ribbon, ink cartridge, or toner unit for your printer and store it in a cool dry place. The first time your current source of print ink starts to run out and you think you have to run to a copy center, you can save the day by snapping in the fresh unit. You will feel like a champion.

PERSONAL DIGITAL ASSISTANTS (PDAs)

Personal Digital Assistants (PDAs) are hand-held devices that generally allow you to enter information on a touch pad with a penlike stylus. Most PDAs offer handwriting recognition as part of the operating system. A PDA screen is about 4 inches by 3 inches, which is a little smaller than two business cards placed side by side. Some have the ability to exchange information with other computers via serial, parallel, and even wireless infrared ports.

Since the Apple Newton's dubious debut in 1993, PDAs have been a polarizing force among personal computer users. One camp reverently believes that one day everyone will be using a PDA for accessing information, recording thoughts, and planning. Others scoff at the notion of a PDA replacing the functions of a portable computer that has real applications, a display that doesn't make one squint, and an actual keyboard for touch-typing. They would rather lug a laptop. A small minority of computer users enjoy these hand-held devices that interpret handwriting, convert currency, manage contact databases and calendars, send faxes, connect to the Internet, tally expense reports, accept pen-based commands, and exchange data with desktop computers.

In addition to being lightweight (1 pound versus 5 to 10 pounds for laptops), PDAs generally have longer battery life than laptops, start up instantly, and automatically save your work.

In addition, keep the following in mind:

- Most of the leading PDAs, such as the Apple MessagePad, US Robotics Pilot, Sharp Zaurus, and Sony Magic Link, come with built-in applications for word processing, phone lists, simple graphics, to-do lists, calendar, and calculator.
- Look for the ability to interface your PDA with external peripherals such as a keyboard. While some PDAs offer either "on screen" keyboards which you tap with your stylus or small fold-down keyboards that resemble calculator-style keys, you will want to add a keyboard to perform any lengthy typing. These add-on keyboards cost $80 to $100.
- The ability to send fax messages is standard with PDAs. The resolution may not be of the highest quality with all applications, but this can be one of the more useful fea-

tures when you need to send printed information for a hotel or meeting confirmation.

■ Not all PDAs have internal modems, but generally, a PDA should accept an external device in the form of a PC card or a regular computer modem. With a modem and the right software, you can connect to online services such as America Online or to your ISP.

SOFTWARE

While the hardware may be more noticeable, software is what allows us to make the hardware accomplish our work and have some fun. Hardware can only process and follow the instructions provided in the lines of code. Think of the hardware as the fancy tray on which the software is served.

Ask a programmer what the most basic unit of software is and she will say a bit. Ask a business person the same question and she will say a file. A file is a self contained grouping of instructions or data or a combination of both.

From a business perspective, you need to make the distinction between three types of files: operating system software, applications, and documents.

Operating System

Without an operating system, your hardware is just a collection of plastic, metal sheets, wires, glass, bits of silicon, a few screws, and a fan. With an operating system, this same collection of components can read and write to its disk drives, play CD-ROMs, display directories, participate on networks, and send output to printers. An operating system, or OS, enables the hardware to perform basic tasks and communicate with peripherals, such as hard drives, CD-ROM players, monitors, scanners, file servers, and printers.

Wintel users—those who run Microsoft Windows on Intel-based or other hardware—have two choices when buying a system today: Windows and Windows NT. For small businesses, Windows 3.1, Windows 95, and Windows 98 are viable systems. Windows NT is Microsoft's operating system for network enterprises in larger business environments. Windows NT is very demanding in terms of RAM, hard drive space, and cpu power, yet it offers greater reliability and the security features required in those environments. For most professional speakers, trainers, and consultants, Windows 95 or 97 will be the ideal choice for Wintel users. If you have already invested time and money in a Windows system, you would do well to upgrade to Windows 95 for the interface improvements over Windows 3.x; newer computers will have the latest version of the operating system software (Windows 98) preinstalled on the hard drive.

Macintosh users—those who run Apple's MacOS on Motorola-based chips—have a similar range of selections. New Mac-compatible systems will run some variation of MacOS 8, though many existing systems are running versions of System 7. Heavy-duty business and network users will want the added reliability and performance of Apple's Rhapsody operating system. For the typical presenter who wants a minimum of fussing with computer hardware and system software, the latest version of Mac OS 8 will provide you with a reliable, versatile system.

Applications

Files that execute instructions are called applications or programs. You are familiar with word processing applications such as Microsoft Word, ClarisWorks, and WordPerfect. These word processors perform tasks that make writing easy, such as managing pagination, remembering margins and tabs, and checking spelling. Other applications you should be familiar with include spreadsheets for calculating project budgets; graphics and page layout programs for designing logos, art-work, and participant materials; presentation software for cre-ating and delivering electronic slide shows; and database applications for managing your contact lists. The word processor will print both what you write and what you receive on your e-mail program. All these categories of appli-cations will be covered in more detail in the next chapter.

The most important aspect to remember about applica-tions is that they produce an output file. The output file of a word processor might be the thank you letter to your last client. The output file of a page layout program might be your quarterly newsletter. The output file from your database might be your master contact list. The output file from any application is generally referred to as a document.

Documents

These documents need to be kept safe or available for editing and reuse, but they exist only temporarily on your hard drive until you back them up. While your operating system, if it is lost, can be reloaded from a CD-ROM (if your system is so equipped) or diskettes, and your applications can be reloaded if you have master copies locked away in a safe place, the work that you create exists only on the hard drive until you back it up. Be sure to follow the guidelines in Chapter 11 for creating a back-up plan and following it to prevent the loss of an important document file.

SUMMARY

Now that you've finished this short course in Computer Technology 101, "tech talk" doesn't have to be a foreign language anymore! If you do run across a word whose meaning you have forgotten, remember to use the glossary at the back of this book. Chapter 2 introduced some of the terminology and concepts you'll find helpful when planning your computer and software purchases, including

■ sizes and types of computer system units (desktop/tower/laptop/notebook);
■ other devices attached to the system unit—monitors, disk drives, keyboards, mice, printers;
■ personal digital assistants (PDAs) as an adjunct to your computer—or even an alternative to a computer;
■ the different types of software on your computer—the operating system, applications, and documents.

In Chapter 3, you'll find out about the most important new way to use your computer—connecting to other computers all over the world using the Internet.

3 Demystifying the Internet

What many people still are not clear about concerning the Internet makes a great deal of difference to how well they can use it. For some, avoiding the Internet is the equivalent of not driving a car at night because no one ever showed them how the headlights work. Here are a few points of clarity to light your way on the information superhighway.

A THUMBNAIL HISTORY OF THE INTERNET

The Internet started out as an experimental project by the U.S. Advanced Research Projects Agency (ARPA) to determine whether a computer communications network could be built to withstand attacks (a necessary contingency during the Cold War era). This project was launched in 1969. The Internet grew rapidly, spreading out to colleges and military research sites over the next 20 years.

Three factors led to the explosive growth of the Internet in the early 1990s. First, in 1989, commercial messages were allowed over the network. Until that time, the Internet was used only for research-related and collegial information exchange because it was not considered proper for the government to subsidize business communications with federal funding. Second, the development of graphical user-interface software called Mosaic, developed for the World Wide Web in 1992, attracted a lot of business attention. For the first time, people working outside the computer and research industry could understand the potential impact of being able to share text and graphics with other people around the world. The third enabling factor that led to the growth of the Internet is the presence of online service providers like America Online, which provided an easy path for the mass market to get online.

WHAT CAN I DO ON THE INTERNET?

The Internet provides the ability to exchange information. What makes the Internet so exciting is that you can pass any type of information on your computer to any other computer on the Internet, and you can do it for the price of a local telephone call. So, if you have a business letter to send, you can send it via e-mail on the Internet. You can also send announcements, digitized pictures, spreadsheets, and short movies, to name a few types of document.

SERVICES OFFERED ON THE INTERNET

What Is E-Mail?

E-mail is electronic messaging—sending and receiving information between computer accounts. The exciting aspect of e-mail is not that information travels well between computer accounts but that people using those accounts can use the information exchange in a variety of creative ways.

Mail systems on computers were around long before the Internet came along because people using computer systems wanted a convenient way to communicate with each other. Few people at the time—if any—considered the possibility of sending messages to a group of 50 million individuals who have e-mail Internet accounts. Remember that 30 years ago, most computers were in large corporations and universities. Even as recently as 1985, fewer than half a million people were exchanging messages via the Internet. Linking computer systems with a common networking scheme enables all of us with Internet e-mail accounts to send mail messages to each other (but not all at once or there would be a terrible traffic jam on the information superhighway).

Many of the activities performed on the Internet are considered "services" to account users. The Internet, logically enough, relies on a system known as a client-server. In a client-server world, the client makes requests of the server and the server returns information to the client after processing the request. With e-mail, client software helps you compose, send, and receive mail. Somewhere else, server software is taking care of transferring e-mail messages to the correct location and storing messages until client software makes a request for them. (Note that a single computer can be its own e-mail station, running both mail client and mail server software, but that's not much fun and is used primarily for learning and testing purposes.) In Chapter 8, you will learn more about sending e-mail that contains more than text messages.

A special case of sending e-mail to an account that is read by an application rather than by a human deserves some discussion here. While it may initially seem terribly sterile to receive a message that was written by a machine (we've all received a letter addressed to "Dear utility consumer . . ."), some of these operations make sense. Mailing lists and autoresponders represent two of these cases.

When you have a large number of people you want to send a message to, you create a mailing list. Compiling the names and addresses is a relatively easy, if not boring, task; what's satisfying about it is knowing that the intended information will reach all of the people on the list. But what if you do not know the names and addresses of the people who need this information? What if you want to open ongoing discussions on a topic and let whoever has an interest in the topic participate in reading about it as well as in contributing to the discussions? Then you create a mailing list and let list-server software manage the process of allowing people to subscribe and unsubscribe from the list. Mailing lists exist for many different topics, such as management practices, running a small business, legal issues, technology products, and hardware/software discussions. On the web site **techedge. BillRingle.com**, you'll find instructions on how to subscribe to some Internet mail lists that you will find useful.

Some mail lists are set up simply to return a message to whoever asks for information, much the same way a recorded phone message works. Internet terminology calls this service an autoresponder. Speakers, consultants, and trainers can use an autoresponder as a way of telling people about the services they offer or where they will be delivering presentations.

The parts of an e-mail address are important to understand. Typically, an e-mail address will have three parts: (1) an account name, (2) the "at" symbol (@), and (3) the Internet address of a host computer. Take "President@White house.gov" as a typical e-mail address.

The account name is the name on a host machine that you use to gain access to the Internet. It is also called your screen name. Accounts are necessary for billing and tracking purposes. In the example above, "President" is the account name. The symbol "@" connects that account with the name of the host computer that receives mail for people who have an account at this address. So "Whitehouse.gov" is the host computer in the system that receives messages. If your name/

account is Joe Nethead, and you are an America Online (AOL) subscriber, your e-mail address might be Nethead@AOL.com.

If you see an "edu" at the end of an e-mail address, you know that the account holder is in an EDUcational environment. If the address ends in "gov," it is a U.S. GOVernmental unit. The "com" suffix means that the address is a COMmercial operation.

 A practice that people develop to send mail to others on the same host (from one AOL account to another AOL account, for example) is to use the intended recipient's screen name only, omitting the rest of the address, such as Ben123 to Patxyz, two AOL accounts. If the person or business is on a different host, you have to use the entire address, such as Ben123@aol.com to PHenry@Earthlink.com, where one person is an AOL and the other is an Earthlink.

What Is the Web?

The web, frequently called the World Wide Web, was created by a researcher named Tim Berners-Lee, who worked at CERN in Switzerland in 1991. Tim was frustrated with two aspects of his work: (1) that scientists working on projects could not easily share documents with scientists working on similar problems but on different computers, and (2) that looking up references cited in a study was so difficult. He realized that networks were prevalent and could provide communication among users if there were a standard language for the various systems. By developing a system which he called hypertext markup language (HTML), he added tags to regular text to give it particular attributes.

His innovation was a very important development. Rather than create special codes to make text look or behave a certain way that differed from one word processing application to another—for example from a DEC host to a Sun host—he now had a common language that could be interpreted in the same way on any mainframe or desktop computer. If you wanted to boldface the word *now* in HTML, you would put the bold tag on either side of the word, like this: <bold>now</bold>. When an HTML browser interpreted and displayed the code, it would simply show the word *now* in boldface type, like this: **now.**

Tim Berners-Lee defined a couple of dozen commands for text attributes, such as bold, italics, different sizes of headings, different types of lists, and so on. He also specified that all graphics would be in one of two common formats: either they would be GIF or JPEG. GIFs are used for line drawings, diagrams, graphs, and other types of illustrations. JPEG images are typically employed when color and detail are more important, such as in scanned images and digital photographs.

Last, Tim showed how links could be created to use a word or phrase on one document to open another document. This process allowed anyone who was reading a research paper on the web to use a hypertext link to jump to another document for background material, then jump back to the original paper.

In short, the World Wide Web is a distributed information system that takes advantage of hypertext links to transmit multimedia content via common network protocols. In English, that means you can see, hear, and interact with web pages from all over the world.

For speakers, trainers, and consultants, the web is a great place to learn, to connect with others, to research topics, to discover background material on clients, to book airline tickets, to reserve cars and hotel rooms, to laugh at jokes, to gather quotations, to assemble case studies, to collect opinions, to find articles, and to do a whole lot more. To begin this adventure, you need a browser and an online connection.

Figure 3.1

Typical Web URL
(Uniform Resource Locator)

```
http://www.Ben1776.com/pages/topics.html
```

A browser is a computer program that allows you to connect to the web. It requests the information you want from a
server, then it interprets and displays the results. A browser is
a wonderful gift. After all, you wouldn't want to have to look
at the raw HTML, would you? To the uninitiated, it is pure
gobbledygook.

To access a web page, you have to make a request to find
a particular web page. The format for doing this is called a
URL (pronounced "you-are-el", not "earl"), which stands for
uniform resource locator.

Let's dissect a typical URL, shown in Figure 3.1, to get a
better understanding of how it works.

The URL has a very flexible structure. The first part is
known as the service. When you enter "http:" you are saying,
"I want to access a web server." HTTP represents Hyper Text
Transfer Protocol and is probably the most common use of
the service prefix. Other common services include: "mailto:"
which initiates an e-mail message, "ftp:" which requests a file
from a server using File Transfer Protocol, and "wais:", which
starts a session for a Wide Area Information Search.

The second part of the URL is the host, separated from the
service by double slashes. Think of the host as the person or
entity inviting guests in to learn about the services or products
being offered. The designation, **www.Ben1776.com** identifies a World Wide Web server for the commercial entity nick-
named Ben1776 (who happens to be Ralph Archbold, CSP,
CPAE, a well-known speaker who presents important business
keynotes in the character of Ben Franklin).

Table 3.1 Common File Types Used with the World Wide Web

File Type Suffix	What This File Type Contains
.gif, .jpeg	graphic files: .gif is usually a graphic, diagram, or drawing .jpeg files are usually photographs
.qt	QuickTime files: for video with audio tracks; the facility to access this format is built into Netscape Navigator and other standard browsers
.ra	RealAudio files: "streaming" audio used to play speeches, music, or news updates without having to wait for the entire audio file to be downloaded

After the host is a pathname, separated from the host by a single slash. The pathname identifies a folder that contains the primary information the host wants you to have. If further information is provided within that folder, a designation for that file follows another single slash.

Web text files usually end in ".html" or ".htm" if the server cannot support the full suffix. Table 3.1 shows other common file suffixes and the file they represent.

How Can I Create My Own Web Page?

Creating web pages requires a basic understanding of hypertext markup language (HTML), a word processor, and a web browser such as Netscape Navigator or Microsoft Internet Explorer. Recall from the introduction of how the web works that various tags, like the bold tag, are placed on either side of a word or phrase in order to "mark up" the way this text is displayed.

CLARIFYING MISCONCEPTIONS

How Do I Log onto the Internet?

You don't, you access it. The Internet is an electronic network that connects your computer to other computers, all of which are connected to the network by modems. The process of logging on involves your gaining that access by connecting to a business enterprise in order to be billed for your measured use of that connection. To log on is to provide that business with an id (identification number or screen name) and a password.

Where Can I Find All of the Good Stuff Online?

The short answer to this question is, "It depends." It depends on what's "good stuff" for you at this moment.

Also, the answer depends on how you got online. If you came in through AOL, you will find an interface that makes exploring as easy as clicking on topic buttons that pique your interest. If you came in through an Internet access provider, you will want to go to the Yahoo! site or one of the search engines to locate sites that cater to your interests.

Are the Internet and the World Wide Web the Same Thing?

No. The Internet is the collection of network hardware (wires, hubs, switches, and routers) using a common set of communications protocols known as TCP/IP. The World Wide Web is a service that is run over the Internet.

Consider this analogy. Imagine the hardwood floor in a high school gym. On that gym floor are lines of different colors. If you wanted to play basketball, you would pay attention to the red lines that define midcourt and the keys. If you wanted to play volleyball, your court would be the green lines outlining the boundaries. And if you were using the gray lines, you would be able to play indoor soccer. The foundation for all these different activities was the same gym floor. That's like the Internet. On top of the same physical infrastructure, you can run different services like e-mail and the World Wide Web.

Why Does a Web Page Look Different on Another Computer?

Your question would be the same if you looked at a movie on a 31-inch surround-sound color TV or watched the same movie on a 10-inch black-and-white portable television.

The chances are that the different computers are using different browsers to view the web pages. The underlying code of the web page hasn't changed, but the way it is being received and the capability of the application to display the graphics and text is a function of the version being used and developer of the web browser.

Will My Computer Catch a Virus from the Internet?

It is unlikely, but take precautions anyway.

Virus programs introduce disruptive code into an operating system or applications—your word processor, for example—but are quite rare. Document viruses, such as the Microsoft Word viruses, the Excel macro virus, or the Merry Christmas virus that infects HyperCard stacks are even less common. Install a virus protection program and know how to eradicate a virus infection in case one should occur.

Do I Need to Worry about Adding E-Mail Addresses?

Yes. The most common ways people get more e-mail addresses is by signing up for an additional ISP, by joining an online service like AOL or CompuServe, by taking a college course in which the instructor assigns you an address for ease of communication, or by receiving an address when an employer assigns you one. In all these cases, another e-mail address is added to the ways people can reach you. The more ways you give people to reach you, the easier and more likely you are to receive communications, right? No! In reality, this approach will drive you crazy. You should try to maintain a single point of contact whenever possible.

SUMMARY

Everyone likes to rhapsodize about the mystique of the Internet, and with good reason. It offers unparalleled opportunities for personal enrichment and business growth. The knowledge you've gained in Chapter 3 can help you turn the "information superhighway" abstraction into concrete understanding—before you hit the online pavement in later chapters. You've learned about

- the history of the Internet and common misconceptions concerning logging on and the perceived lack of safety;
- the World Wide Web, an important service on the Internet; and
- how the Internet connects to you, and how you can be located on it through your e-mail address.

Now that you know some basics about the Internet, you'll learn in subsequent chapters what you need to get connected. In Part Two you'll learn how to go online using a commercial online service or an Internet service provider.

■ Look at a business card or promotional piece you've received recently and find the e-mail address on it. Circle and name the three parts of an e-mail address.

■ Analyze a published web address the same way.

■ Define the following terms:

    client

    server

    autoresponder

    browser

4 AOL—The Best Choice for You?

You may be wondering why America Online (AOL) is the preferred service among speakers. After all, aren't there other public online services, such as CompuServe, MSN, and Prodigy? Let's look at the four reasons you will find more speakers, trainers, and consultants on AOL than on any of the other services.

First, consider its size. With membership of 8 million and growing as of early 1997, AOL is by far the largest commercial online service. CompuServe, its nearest competitor, has fewer than 2 million members. In a survey conducted for this book of 1267 American Society for Training and Development and National Speakers Association members, I found that 58.9 percent of the group used AOL as their primary e-mail address, 30.6 percent subscribed to an Internet service provider, and 10.5 percent connected via CompuServe.

Second, AOL aggressively promotes its services, mailing out trial subscription disks, including them in magazines, and encouraging members to sign up their friends. The available setup disks are a convenience when you are looking for an online service to join. While it is annoying and frustrating to receive busy signals when trying to log onto the service because of a growing membership, busy signals simply indicate that the demand at that time for inbound modems exceeds the supply of modems on hand at the location you are dialing. AOL keeps adding new modems to meet the demand.

Next, consider the resources you'll find on each service. Chat rooms, areas where people can gather and exchange typed messages with each other, are used regularly by members of the National Speakers Association (NSA) and American Society for Training and Development (ASTD). Databases of relevant periodicals are available for research. While CompuServe also has excellent online databases to search, it is not as friendly as AOL for first-time users.

Look at the widespread access available to AOL members. A technical group within AOL, called ANS, manages America Online's network services. (At press time, World Com has moved to acquire both AOL's ANS and the networking infrastructure of CompuServe's online service.) ANS has designed, installed, and run the world's largest data communications network, supporting more than 160,000 modems in 472 U.S. cities and an additional 152 cities internationally. By using the ANS network, AOL extends the ability to dial into its service using a local number to approximately 85 percent of the U.S. population. For those outside the local calling areas, AOL offers an 800 number for access, for which subscribers pay a premium. For the cost of a local phone call in just about any major city, you can access your e-mail from a hotel, reply to a message, or look up information about a desired topic.

Finally consider AOL's support. If you have trouble connecting, you can call an 800 number 24 hours a day, seven days a week. If you are connected, you can use an online chat room to ask a technician a question and get an immediate response.

Price isn't an issue because all online services offer similar unlimited plans at about the same monthly fee. Table 4.1 on pages 46 and 47 gives a summary of the four largest commercial online services at the time of publication. It includes pricing plans for U.S. subscribers, advantages of the service, and disadvantages of the service.

SUGGESTED STEPS TO GETTING OFF ON THE RIGHT FOOT

With any online service, you will encounter challenges in connecting, when traveling, and in locating information.

In this section, you will learn some of the general tips for signing on with a commercial online service. The next chapter covers tips for making the most of your AOL connection.

Tip #1

If you have not tried any of the services, send away for a couple of the free sign-up kits by calling the toll-free numbers in Table 4.1 and telling the customer service representative what kind of computer and which operating system you are using. The major commercial online services offer free trial periods. It is in the service's best interest to make it as easy, fun, and productive an experience for prospective members as possible. It is in your best interest to give each of the services a try.

Tip #2

Once you get the kits, take the services for a test drive. Search their forums and databases. Test out examples that make sense for your work and interests. Send test messages to your own screen name to experiment with their mail software. Read on for more useful exercises in Chapter 5.

Table 4.1   Comparing the Commercial Online Services

	Pricing Plans for U.S. Subscribers	Advantages	Disadvantages
America Online (AOL)	■ $19.95 per month flat rate dial-up, unlimited usage ■ Senior citizen discounts, annual prepayment discounts available ■ $9.95 per month flat rate through an ISP, unlimited usage ■ $4.95 per month for 3 hours base, plus $2.50 per hour over base	■ Rich content, well-organized channels of information ■ Easy-to-use "client" (program used to access the service) ■ Extensive library of freeware and shareware ■ Monitored discussion groups ■ Chat capability for live conversations and group discussions ■ Emphasis on creating online "community" atmosphere ■ Capable technical support available via phone and online	■ Can be difficult to access during peak hours ■ Service areas can be "temporarily unavailable" ■ Technical support may sometimes exhibit unhelpful attitude
CompuServe*	■ $24.95 per month for 10 hours base, plus $1.95 per hour over base ■ $9.95 per month for 5 hours, plus $2.95 per hour additional time	■ Excellent online library of searchable databases ■ Presence of many hardware, software vendors for support forums	■ Cryptic numeric user names used for log in and e-mail addresses (easier-to-remember aliases are available) ■ Cumbersome overhead for client software adds delays ■ Many content areas have additional entry and hourly usage costs

	Pricing Plans for U.S. Subscribers	Advantages	Disadvantages
The Microsoft Network (MSN)	■ $19.95 per month unlimited access ■ $6.95 per month for 5 hours, plus $2.50 per hour additional time ■ $6.95 per month flat rate through an ISP, unlimited usage	■ Actually a hybrid service, since its content is entirely web-based ■ Can provide ISP services if needed ■ Excellent support for Microsoft products	■ Client software available only for Windows 95 ■ Offers much editorial content, but little reference content ■ Restricts use of e-mail package to Microsoft Exchange ■ Some overdesigned layouts make for confusing navigation ■ Other vendors (especially competitors) are not represented
Prodigy Internet	■ $19.95 per month unlimited access ■ $10 per month for 10 hours, plus $2.50 per hour additional time	■ Was first online service to integrate the World Wide Web ■ Offers editorial content and community connection opportunities	■ Still heavily commercialized, with ads on service "pages" ■ Unlike other services, does not offer extensive support forums for Microsoft or other computer hardware or software vendors (though links to company web sites are provided)

* At press time, AOL has moved to acquire the CompuServe online services, subscribers, and content. Their plan is to maintain CompuServe as a distinct brand and service.

Tip #3

Do not tell people to send you mail at a temporary address/screen name on a particular service. Wait until you have settled on a primary service and then let the world know where to reach you. Some commercial online services do not allow automatic forwarding outside their service, which makes it difficult to "leave a forwarding address" when you move on. Having to check multiple locations for e-mail is unnecessarily time consuming at best and risks reliability and your reputation at its worst.

Tip #4

If you have a computer that travels, be sure to load it with the software you choose. Whether you pick AOL, Compu-Serve, MSN, or Prodigy, you will want the capability to log in from a hotel or other remote location, just as you would from your office. Take the time to install the software and config-ure it at your office, where you have the time to test the con-figuration. For security reasons, it's recommended that you not save your sign-on password on computers that leave your office in case of theft or tampering.

Tip #5

Download local access numbers on an as-needed basis before you leave for a trip. Access numbers are the telephone num-bers that you have the computer dial on a modem to connect to an online service. Preparation will pay off when you quickly need to access your mail or look up an article from off site. Your online service will provide you a list of access numbers in the cities that are lay-over stops on nonstop air-line trips!

SUMMARY

Even if you've heard all the press coverage about problems in the online service world and the shakeout among online providers, there are many reasons why an online service is right for you. Chapter 4 has made the case for commercial online services as an important tool for trainers, speakers, and consultants, teaching you

- facts about the four major commercial online services, including pricing, advantages, and disadvantages;
- why AOL makes sense as the online service of choice for speakers, trainers, and consultants;
- what to keep in mind when you try before you buy with free trial software.

Are you ready to take the plunge and go online? Chapter 5 covers the basics of using America Online.

 Call and order two COS (Commercial Online Service) start-up kits. Try them for 30 days and compare the value of the services and resources offered for your business needs and personal interests.

What to Do Once You're Logged On

To get online initially, you need four items: a computer, a modem, a phone line, and client software to access the online service.

If you are self-employed or otherwise entrepreneurially minded, having a telephone goes with the territory. One recommendation I make to those who are making a living from their speaking work is to get a separate phone line for your online communications. If you have a fax line, you could use it for both your fax machine and modem.

There are two critical reasons why you should not tie up your voice line. First, you don't want to have potential clients get a busy signal. Second, there will be times when you want to be online and talking to someone on the phone at the same time.

GETTING SIGNED UP ON AOL

America Online (AOL) uses special software to connect to its online services. Here's how to get a free copy of the client software kit.

1. Call AOL and request a kit for your operating system: Windows 95, Windows 3.1, Macintosh, or MS-DOS. Call the customer service department at (800) 827-6364 and tell the operator what kind of computer you are using and where to send the disk.

2. Ask a friend who is an AOL member to send you a kit. That friend will get online credit for helping you join. For every new recruit, the member gets a credit of five online hours as a thank you from AOL.

When you have the modem connected to your computer and plugged into the second phone line and the AOL software is installed on your computer, you are ready to log on for the first time. Have a credit card ready to help complete the registration.

Here is the information you will be asked to provide when you register:

- name
- address
- phone
- user name and password
- payment method (such as credit card) and choice of billing plan
- acceptance of AOL's terms of service (TOS)

The requirements for your name, address, and phone are straightforward.

Selecting a User Name

A screen name is what identifies you as a user on a particular system. Once your user name is confirmed, you can send and receive e-mail from that account. You will want to publish that screen name widely, so anyone with Internet access— whether they get it on AOL or not—can exchange mail with you. The format in which you will share your AOL account name is as follows: "AOLname@aol.com." Simply substitute the AOL name you have chosen for the AOLname in the example. A consultant with the screen name "Rodgers" would tell people to send mail to "Rodgers@aol.com" to reach her.

When you select a screen name (also known as a user name), pay attention to three criteria. First, your screen name has to be unique among all the existing screen names on America Online. Second, the name you select cannot be longer than 10 characters. Third, it should either reinforce your name or reflect some memorable and/or distinct aspect of your business. Let's take a look at each of these areas.

The reason your screen name has to be unique is that when AOL gets mail, either from another AOL user or from someone else on the Internet, the computer has to know without a doubt for whom that mail is destined.

All mail systems, whether on AOL or elsewhere on the Internet, forbid special symbols and characters because of the way message addresses are handled. On AOL, you can use upper or lower case letters, numbers, and spaces as long as you follow a few rules.

1. The screen name must begin with a letter, which will automatically be capitalized. Thus, if Bob Pike, an expert on interactive training, entered "pike" as a screen name and it was not in use already, "Pike" would become his official screen name. Even though AOL starts every screen name with a capital, it doesn't make a distinction between upper- and lowercase letters when routing mail to a screen name. Mail sent to "pike@aol.com", "Pike@aol.com", "PIKE@aol.com", and even "PiKe@aol.com" would all go to the same user.

2. Don't put a space in your screen name. A common practice for selecting a screen name is to use your first name and last name run together. By capitalizing the first letter of each name, the word is more readable. Under this approach, Zig Ziglar could become "ZigZiglar" on AOL. (In the unusual event that someone else has claimed this screen name, he could attempt "ZiglarZig" or "ZZiglar" or

"ZiglarZ" as alternatives.) AOL allows up to nine characters in a screen name.

3.   AOL prohibits the use of special characters in screen
     names, such as underscores, periods, and dashes. Other
     ISPs offer more flexibility in this regard. On AOL, how-
     ever, you can certainly address mail to people on other
     systems and use these special characters in the mail
     addresses you use.

Why is your user name so important? First, visibility. Your
e-mail address will be on your business cards, brochures, sta-
tionery, proposals, newsletters, articles, books, and web pages.
You want it to be easy to recognize as being associated with
you or your business.

Second, ease of use. You want an e-mail address that is
easy to read as well as easy to say. When a client is sending
an inquiry via e-mail by reading your address from your
brochure, you don't want to risk a typing error. CompuServe
accounts are the worst offenders of this principle, with their
strict numeric accounts: who can tell whether the account
you were sending to was supposed to be 33456.0876@Com-
puServe.com or 33456.0786@CompuServe.com? (In late 1996,
CompuServe allowed its users to claim user names with letters and receive mail to the "letter name" accounts. However,
mail sent from these accounts is still marked as coming from
the "numeric" user name.)

With AOL screen names, you have 10 characters to work
with, so use them well. Glenna Salsbury, an NSA leader and
nationally known speaker and consultant, uses an account
name linked to her business, "ISpeak4You". A former LAPD
detective sergeant now specializing in travel safety training,
Kevin Coffey, goes by the address "StopThief@aol.com". If
you receive mail from "JustJoking@aol.com", you will be in
contact with the irrepressible comedian Dale Irvin.

Guidelines for AOL screen names:

- Use 10 alphanumeric characters
- Avoid the use of spaces
- First character must be a letter and will be uppercase
- Make good use of upper- and lowercase letters
- Reinforce your name or business
- Make the name easy to read and easy to speak

I'M ON AOL. NOW WHAT?

As a new user of AOL's Online Commercial Service (OCS), you have much to learn about the services available to you as well as about the vast information resources that you can now access.

Here are 7 first steps for any speaker, trainer, or consultant who wants to get up the learning curve as quickly as possible. If you are already online, you can use the following steps as a checklist to make sure you are making the most of your time online.

1. Complete your online profile
2. Send e-mail
3. Ask for help online
4. Find and download free software
5. Mark your favorite places
6. Look up information on a topic
7. Browse the web

1. Complete Your Online Profile

An online profile is a short description of you and your interests. Remember that AOL has an extremely diverse membership—from a meeting planner in Atlanta to a bagel shop owner in San Francisco to a fly fisherman in Minnesota to an Air Force pilot in Germany who wants to stay in touch with her family in Colorado Springs to a sixth grader in Ohio who likes to play chess after school.

For you as a speaker, trainer, or consultant, this diverse membership constitutes either information you can use in your work or people you can service. You want to give helpful information about yourself to anyone who queries the AOL membership database about your expertise and availability. You will be able to enter up to 250 characters per line, including letters, numbers, spaces, and punctuation, using several categories.

To start, pull down the Members menu and select the Member Directory command. This will show the Member Directory screen, as shown in Figure 5.1.

You have the opportunity to fill in each of these areas: hobbies, occupation, computers used, and personal quote. Although only about 100 characters will fit on screen, you

Figure 5.1

AOL Member Directory Screen

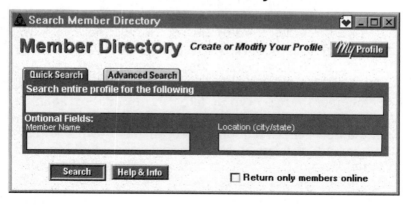

can continue typing because each field holds up to 250 characters.

Here are a few tips on how to use these fields to your advantage.

- Use keywords and meaningful phrases rather than sentences. "Sales training professional, New Jersey, racquetball" is more efficient and will lead to just as many positive hits as "I am a sales training professional who lives in New Jersey and plays racquetball on weekends to relax." Prepositions and pronouns are rarely used as criteria when people are trying to find someone.

- If you are a member of the National Speakers Association (NSA) or the American Society for Training and Development (ASTD), be sure to include these as occupation keywords. Meeting planners know to look for professional affiliations as a screening mechanism.

- Be focused. List your primary areas of expertise so that someone who sees this short list will know for sure that you are a likely match for a presentation need. In addition to focusing on your top priorities, be sure to list the root words and common variations in your profile. For example, include *selling* as well as *sales,* add *training, trainer,* and *trains* for maximum exposure.

- Include other professional attributes under the occupation field, such as "writer,""author," "radio/TV guest," "expert witness," "model," and so on. You can list these items on any of the lines because a search for keywords will include the hobby, occupation, computers used, and quotation fields.

- Remember that you can update this information at any time. If you join a new association, publish a new book, find a new gem of a quotation, or upgrade your computer system, add this information so that people looking for others who match these key characteristics will find you.

Click the OK button to save your up-to-date member profile information.

2. Send E-Mail

One of the most important advantages of getting online is to send and receive e-mail, so it's important to get a good start. First, you will send a test message to yourself. Then you will learn to send a message through the Internet to another address. But first, compare e-mail with postal mail.

Sending a message via e-mail is a lot like sending a letter in the mail. You have to tell the system who the message is for and who it is from and also include a message. However, you can't beat its convenience. You can send or read e-mail in the comfort of your home office without having to wait for the letter carrier, walk out to the mail box at the foot of your driveway, or drive to the post office.

How E-Mail Differs from Post Office Mail

E-mail differs from post office mail in four ways. First, e-mail is faster and more reliable than post office mail. The speed is obvious when you can send a message to someone via e-mail and have it arrive in seconds, whether that person is across town or across the international dateline. Hand-carried letters, playfully referred to by e-mail users as snail mail, cannot match this delivery. However, new and inexperienced users often complain that e-mail is less dependable because they have sent mail to the wrong person by mistake or because the person they sent mail to lost their message accidentally. These problems are caused not by faults of the system but by the carelessness of the users. Later on, you will learn about how to avoid the most common errors in corresponding via e-mail.

Second, e-mail is easier and cheaper to send to large numbers of people than is postal mail. Because e-mail can be forwarded to huge mailing lists (either deliberately or accidentally), be mindful of what you write, especially about other individuals and other organizations. Another way of saying this is never put anything in an e-mail message that you wouldn't want to read about in the newspaper tomorrow.

Third, e-mail is easier to redistribute than is postal mail. With a couple of keystrokes, you can forward a message you have received to one or a hundred recipients, adding appropriate comments to that message.

Fourth, e-mail can be accessed at any time of the day and from any connection point. In addition to connecting to your AOL account via your office, you can also check on mail and reply to messages from any hotel room or conference center that has a phone line. Usually, the only cost from a large city is a local call to a nearby AOL point of presence.

How to Send E-Mail

In this exercise, you will send a short message to yourself, simply to demonstrate how e-mail works. If you have accomplished a level of proficiency beyond this, feel free to skip to the next section.

1. Connect to AOL.
2. Pull down the Mail menu and select the Compose Mail command. You will see a window like the one in Figure 5.2.
3. Type material in the blank spaces:
    a. In the "To:" field, type in your screen name.
    b. Type "Mail to Self" or another message in the Subject space.
    c. Type a short but unique message in the message body space.

    For example, here is text that we sometimes use for testing e-mail in a seminar I teach called Driver's Ed for the Information Superhighway: "This is a test message. In the event of a real message, you would find interesting and perhaps even useful content in this place."
4. After you have completed your message, click the Send Now button. AOL will confirm what you did with the

Figure 5.2

Compose Mail Window in AOL

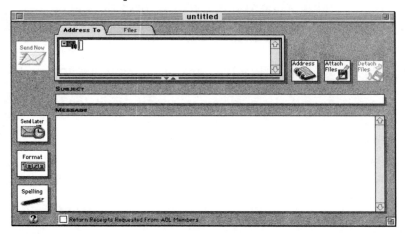

Macintosh

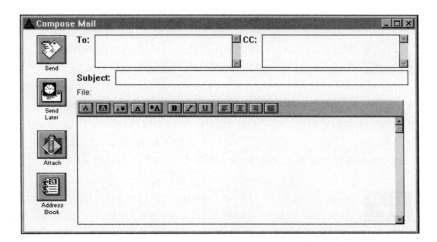

Windows

message: "Your mail has been sent." Click the OK button. (The Send Later button is for queuing messages off line, then sending when you become connected.) You are connected already, so now you can immediately check your mail to retrieve the mail you sent. To do this, pull down the Mail menu again and select Read New Mail. The New Mail box will list the letter to yourself. Double-click on it, and you will be able to read that message. You may then keep it as a new letter, delete it, or exit the dialog box.

Exercise

As an additional exercise, you can send mail to an automatic mail program for readers of this book. These programs are called auto responders or mailbots (mail robots).

From AOL, select the compose mail command and address a message to "TechEdge@BillRingle.com". In the body of the message, write the word *Hello* and send it. When the autoresponder software receives your e-mail, it will send a message back to verify your message was received.

TECH TIP *You can compose mail offline (without actually being logged on to AOL) and then sign on to send it. This technique is both efficient and convenient whether you have several messages to send, or one of your messages is long or requires a lot of careful thought, or you are traveling and want to compose it one place (such as at 35,000 feet) and send it from another (such as on the eighth floor of a Hyatt Hotel).*

TECH TIP *Attaching files to mail messages is a very useful and valuable skill to develop. No other method can get an electronic file to someone as fast.*

Don Blohowiak, an international business consultant and speaker, needed to send a PowerPoint slide show to a client in Slovenia. He needed to send the master copy of the worksheets and PowerPoint presentation file to the workshop coordinator.

Just before leaving for the airport, he was able to send the necessary files via an e-mail attachment. His contact received the files without a problem. When Don arrived, the materials had been printed and were waiting for him, saving him the time, energy, and cost associated with printing and shipping the materials.

On AOL, you can attach files easily by clicking the Attach Files button. You will be presented with a standard open file dialog box, where you can navigate to the location on your hard drive where the file you want to send resides. After you select a file to be attached, the name of the file and its size will appear in the field next to the Attach Files button. If you change your mind and do not want to send a file with the message you are creating, you can select the file name in the field and click the Detach File button. When sending files from an AOL account to another AOL account, the total size of the files can reach up to 15.8 MB. When sending to someone on the Internet outside AOL, you are restricted to 1 MB.

3. Ask for Help Online

Another significant difference between a commercial online service and an Internet service provider is that a commercial service offers greater levels of support. AOL members can call (800) 827-6364 seven days a week if they are having trouble connecting to the service for any reason. If, for example, you have acquired a new modem and need to change settings to connect, call that number. Do the same when you are calling from a hotel and you need the local access number.

Once you are connected to the service, AOL offers another level of support—interactive chat rooms with technicians. Trained support people are available to answer your questions and solve your problems. These support technicians, however, are rarely waiting around. They are usually dealing with several other members at the same time.

For an overview of how the online chat support works, think of a deli counter. A certain number of people can walk up to the "help counter" at one time. The support technician asks how she or he can help a member on a first-come, first-serve basis. After resolving one person's issues, the support technician then engages the next person. Sometimes, the support technician may instruct the first person to try changing some setting on his computer, then come back and tell the technician whether the suggestion solved the problem.

> **TECH TIP** *Use keywords to navigate from one area of AOL to another. To access the keyword dialog box, pull down the Go To menu and select the Keyword command (or use the keyboard equivalent shown on the pull-down menu). After entering a keyword, press the Return key.*
>
> *Keep your eyes open for keywords located in the bottom right corner of many screens. Not all AOL areas are linked by a keyword, but many are, and they can save you time.*

To enter the support area, pull down the Help menu and select Online Support or use the keyword *help*. AOL provides three distinct areas to get help, each with its own staff and hours.

- General help
- Technical help staff
- Pricing plan information

Each of these chat areas takes place in an online "auditorium."

Help with general questions about AOL as well as technical difficulties are responded to seven days a week, from 7 A.M. to 2:45 A.M. EST. Answers to questions about AOL's pricing plans are also available every day of the week, but only from 8 A.M. to MIDNIGHT.

The general area for participating in chat sessions is the People Connection. Be forewarned that many of the conversations that take place here are strictly social in nature and of low business value. Perhaps one of the best activities you can arrange to learn the value of an AOL chat is to meet a friend in a private chat room (also available from the People Connection screen) and have a real-time online conversation.

TECH TIP *Log your chat session. When you log your chat session, you save it to disk, rather than let it scroll off into oblivion. Many times, people will pass along tips and insights that make a better impression when they are reread than when a chat is happening live.*

To log a chat session, pull down the File menu and select the Log Manager, shown in Figure 5.3.

Figure 5.3

AOL Log Manager

Macintosh

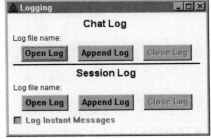

Windows

So much information is available on the Internet—some of it coming to you in huge quantities—that you don't always have time to read it as it arrives. AOL has provided a feature called logging. When the log command is turned on, all the incoming text is recorded on your hard disk. You can then access it at your leisure when the online clock isn't running by opening it on any word processor or on AOL.

Using the Log Manager, you can create a new log file at any time or append information to existing files in any of three categories:

■ *System logs capture the text from every screen you visit. This log is useful when you go from one AOL screen to another because it can save you a great deal of time making notes and copying and pasting material. However, the disk file can become gigantic in very little time. Do not leave System logging on by default!*

■ *Chat logs capture all of the text sent by participants in a chat session. Luckily, every comment made is attributed to the person's screen name making the comment. Be sure to turn on your Chat log before you enter a chat room for a discussion or you are likely to miss some important exchanges. However, if you remember that you want to keep a log in the middle of a discussion, remember that you can access your log manager at any time and begin recording to a chat log file.*

■ *Instant messages are useful for people who spend enough time on AOL that friends and associates know to find you there online. When they do, they can send you an instant message (IM). Most IM's are of trivial lasting value. Few business people would want to save a "Hi, meet me in the chat room in 2 minutes" type of message to a log file.*

TECH TIP *Know the abbreviations used in e-mail and chat sessions. The Internet has not only a great deal of technical lingo but social conventions as well.*

Here is a list of some of the most popular symbols and abbreviations that you will encounter online. You may also hear these symbols referred to as emoticons.

In this first group, cock your head to the left to properly interpret the symbol.

```
:-)    =    smile
:-D    =    big grin
;-)    =    wink
:*     =    kiss
:X     =    my lips are sealed
:P     =    sticking out tongue
{}     =    a hug
:(     =    frown
:'(    =    crying
```

This second group encompasses commonly used abbreviations. For instance, you might read in a message: "This joke will have you ROTFL."

```
LOL   =    Laughing Out Loud
ROTFL =    Rolling On The Floor Laughing
AFK   =    Away From Keyboard
BAK   =    Back At Keyboard
BRB   =    Be Right Back
TTFN  =    Ta-Ta For Now!
WB    =    Welcome Back
GMTA  =    Great Minds Think Alike
BTW   =    By The Way
IMHO  =    In My Humble Opinion
WTG   =    Way To Go!
```

4. Find and Download Free Software

Access to free and low-cost software is one of the most exciting benefits of being online. Downloading from AOL software
archives offers some protections against viruses not available
on open Internet sites.

The advantages of downloading software are compelling:
you get access to far more software than any computer store
could ever carry on its shelves; you can use software that performs simple tasks or makes modifications to existing software (sometimes called a "hack") that was never intended to
become a commercial product but is really useful; and you
get to "try before you buy" a wide range of commercial and
noncommercial software.

Public domain software includes programs, templates, and
hacks that the author wants credit, but no money, for creating. The software developer is truly altruistic: "I wrote this
because I thought it was useful, cool, or fun and now I want
to share it with the world."

Shareware is freely distributable, noncommercial software
that was developed by individual programmers or by software
companies. If you continue to use it after a stated trial period,
you are asked to pay the requested fee.

To access the AOL software library, click on the Computers and Software channel, then click on the Software Center
button, or use the keyword *File Search* to go directly to the
search screen, which contains a form. The form allows you to
select from date ranges of when the file you are looking for
was posted to AOL. You can select from "all dates," the "past
month," or the "past week" if you believe it was a very recent
posting. In addition, you can narrow the scope of the search
to a particular software category such as graphics, communications, help desk information, utilities, or business software.

If you are looking for a file of a particular name, simply
type that file into the search definition field. For example,

you could type `stuffit` into the field to find the latest version of one of the most popular and useful utilities for file compression for both Macintosh and Windows users.

If you want a software program that will help you manage your checkbook, type `checkbook` in the Search Definition space. AOL will return a list of the first 20 software files available for download. In that overview list, you will see the software category, the subject, and the filename. If any of these pieces of information catch your interest, you can get more details on the file by clicking the Read Description button. You can also choose to download the file now or to add the file to a list to download at a later time. Postponing downloads is a good idea when you have multiple files to bring down to your computer. This technique is explained in greater detail in the "FlashSessions/Automatic AOL" tip.

In addition to the general software library, you should know about the particular company support areas on AOL. You can browse the Computers and Software area labeled Company Connection. You can go directly to a company support area, where you will find answers to common questions about products and technical support as well as about software to download.

As a speaker, trainer, or consultant, you might choose Companies by Category to see what presentation software is available to increase your effectiveness. With a double-click, choose the category Graphics/Presentations, and you can secure information about presentation graphics produced by more than three dozen companies. Each company will supply product information, customer support, and information about purchasing its products.

Exercise
Download Adobe Acrobat Reader from the Adobe company support area. Use the keyword *Adobe* to find the support

area. Then click the line in the scrolling field which references the Acrobat Reader. More and more companies are using the Acrobat format (also known as PDF, for Portable Document Format) as a way of distributing electronic file content which can be read with a high degree of precision layout (unlike a plain text document) on Windows, Macintosh, or Unix computers.

TECH TIP *Many times, files are compressed before they are uploaded to the AOL host computer to save time transferring as well as to save storage space. When you download a compressed file, your primary concern should be how you will uncompress it so you can work with it. Fortunately, two factors are working in your favor. First, common standards of compression make file decompression a fairly straightforward routine on either the Windows or Macintosh platforms. Most Windows files are compressed in a "zip" format; Most Mac files are "stuffed." The second factor in your favor as an AOL user is that platform-appropriate decompression software is built into the AOL client software. So as a file download reaches completion, the next logical step of uncompressing it is automatically carried out by AOL.*

5. Mark Your Favorite Places

With so many interesting and useful places to visit on AOL, it becomes a challenge to return to your favorite places, unless you mark them. By designating a screen as one of your "favorite places," you can organize a custom "map" through the vast AOL information space.

You will learn this technique in the next few paragraphs, and it will become one of the most useful tools in your online repertoire. Every time you come to a screen you want to "remember" for later visits, click on the heart symbol in

Figure 5.4

AOL Favorite Places Screen

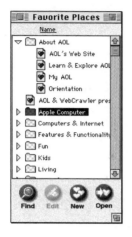

Macintosh   **Windows**

Copyright 1997 America Online; Used by Permission.

the upper right corner of the screen. To access and manipulate the list you create, use the Go To menu and select the Favorite Places command (see Figure 5.4).

Here are some of the finer points of Favorite Places.

■ Favorite places act like keywords in that they take you directly to a particular screen. While some screens can be tagged with a keyword, more screens have the Favorite Places heart icon.

■ Favorite places can be easily managed from the Favorite Places screen even when you are offline. To move a favorite place file into a different folder, you simply drag it from one location to another. To delete a defunct Favorite Place, you simply highlight the favorite place listing and press the Delete key on your keyboard. To create a new folder for Favorite Places, you click the New button

at the bottom of the scrolling field. You will be presented
with a choice to create a new Favorite Place, in which
case you type in the URL or AOL keyword, or to create a
new folder, in which case you type in the name for the
new folder.

■ In the Macintosh version of AOL, you can locate buried
or forgotten favorites by using the Find button. Later versions of the Windows client software will probably
include this feature.

■ If you are offline, you can double-click on a Favorite Place
file. Doing so will launch AOL, Connect if possible, and
bring up the desired screen.

6. Look Up Information on a Topic

Online communication allows you not only to send information out into the world as you do with e-mail but also to
reach out for information that others have made available.
America Online organizes and stores information in its databases, which are available to members only. CompuServe also
has valuable database information and articles. If you cannot
find what you need on AOL, CompuServe is definitely worth
browsing because these commercial online resources are likely
to be better organized than other Internet sites.

Let's look at four examples of how to search for different
types of information on AOL for business topics. In Part
Three you will learn more about searching for information
effectively on the Internet.

Use the Digital Library

Running down to the local library after 9 P.M. to look up a
few facts for a presentation is just not likely unless you are a
college student and your library is open that late. Visiting the
New York Public Library on the spur of the moment is just
not possible for most readers. However, what if a section of

the reference desk of the New York Public Library was available at no additional cost, open 24 hours a day, and accessible from the comfort of your home office? It is—through America Online.

To get to this digital library, click on the Reference channel (or use the keyword *SuperLibrary*). Macmillan Publishing sponsors the library's presence and offers several other resources in addition to the reference desk. Here, you can browse or search for information on such topics as famous quotations, conversion factors, world maps, and historical facts.

For example, say that you are customizing a presentation for an international meeting and you want to weave in an example using a famous painter or sculptor from Britain. Go ahead, name one. Stumped? Go to the SuperLibrary and you can browse through the cultural section, which is arranged by country of the artist, and there you will find a list of well-known names to draw upon for your talk.

In the Reference area, you will also find such valuable resources as

- a thesaurus
- English usage guides
- the *American Psychological Association (APA) Style Guide*
- the *Modern Language Association (MLA) Style Guide*
- quotation databases
- Que's Computer Glossary

It is true that you could own hardcopy editions of these works, but searching electronically is much easier and is likely to turn up more current information in many cases.

Use Hoovers Company Index

When you want to learn about the products, people, and markets of the largest public and private companies in the

United States, turn to Hoovers (Keyword: *Hoovers*). It offers concise, complete summary information on companies that allows you to get a sense of their business products, recent sales, officers, and corporate resources. For the speaker, trainer, or consultant addressing this market, Hoovers is the Cliff Notes of corporate background information.

For example, a business consultant once compared the success Paul Allen has had with his software company, Asymetrix, to that of his friend and cofounder of Microsoft, Bill Gates. A quick check on Hoovers showed the difference in revenue (little surprise) as well as staff (big surprise): Microsoft employed more than twenty thousand people; Asymetrix employed fewer than a hundred. The difference he discovered caused the consultant to rework an important section of his speech. It's better for your credibility to check your facts in advance rather than to follow up when you have made an error or significant omission. When the basics are at your client's fingertips as easily as they are your own, it is simply a part of being a professional.

Ask Others Online for Their Ideas

Nothing shows you've done your homework on a company more thoroughly than having personal stories from the organization or community that support your message. For instance, if you were visiting a city for a convention, you could find out what the relevant issues of the day were by reading the local newspapers or interviewing some of the local convention attendees. If the city you were visiting was one of the Digital Cities on AOL, you could read about what's hot and interview people online about those issues that were current and that intersected with your message.

Use the Major News Sources

If you were looking for examples of computer break-ins that a general business audience could relate to, one place to start would be @times, the New York Times area in the News-Stand Channel on AOL. Here you would find an interview between @times editor Elliott Rebhun and writer John Markoff. Markoff had just written a book about tracking and catching computer thief Kevin Mitnick and was responding to questions by Elliot and other questions that had been forwarded by AOL members who were "listening in" on the chat in the AOL auditorium.

Here is a brief sample of that interview to give you an idea of the process of a chat interview as well as the quality of information available in the AOL archives.

As you read this interview, think about

- how you can use the examples given as part of a presentation,
- how you can adapt some of the questions to your next interview, and
- whether you would find value asking questions during such an online interview.

In addition to @times, you can visit other online newspapers and magazines in the NewsStand Channel, read or search breaking news stories from Reuters or other sources in Today's News (keyword: *news*), and look for auditorium and chat events that might be of interest to you at AOL Live (keyword: *live*). AOL Live also maintains a searchable archive of auditorium transcripts.

```
ElliottNYT : PaulJK1 wonders: Is there a
movie in the works? It would make a good
one.

MarkoffNYT : There is a movie, I think.
Miramax has purchased the rights to "Take-
down," and some screenwriters are working
on a script. I have no idea whether it
will ever make it to the screen, however.
```

ElliottNYT : If you've just joined us, our
guest tonight is New York Times technology
correspondent John Markoff. What progress
if any is being made in improving Internet
security against intruders like Mitnick?

MarkoffNYT : It's actually a fairly disap-
pointing situation. The technology exists
to make the Internet tremendously more
secure, but because of export control laws
and simple laziness on the part of systems
providers, the software and hardware is
not yet in place. Ideally, good security
should be available and directly embedded
in the user's personal computer transparently. It's technically possible, but there
hasn't been a huge demand for it yet.

ElliottNYT : Cases like Mitnick's clearly
make much of the public wary about the
Internet. Albert Dover asks: Is it reasonably safe to engage in financial transactions
like buying and selling stocks over the
Net? Are some browsers safer than others?

MarkoffNYT : Buying and selling stocks is
a really interesting application, and one
that I would think seriously about before
jumping in. On the other hand I would have
no difficulty using my credit card over the
Net. It's pretty obvious that there is no
more risk there than using your credit
card in a restaurant. But before I put my
life savings on the Net, I would want some
fairly strong guarantees from the service
provider. I don't know if they are being
provided yet. One issue that I think
hasn't been addressed adequately is the
aggregation of financial data on central-

ized server computers that are reasonably
exposed and connected to the Net. My guess
is that there will be some horror stories
before that technology matures.

ElliottNYT : Another question on on-line
commerce from LSchnei781: Do you have an
E-cash account? Any insights or warnings
about this kind of commerce on the Internet?

MarkoffNYT : I do use a credit card occa-
sionally to buy books and software, but so
far that's all. I'm really pretty skepti-
cal about proprietary systems that require
you to establish a separate account for
each different merchant. It's going to
take a while, I imagine, before there are
broad standards that will make it as easy
to buy and sell on the Net as in the real
world.

Excerpt from The New York Times on America Online Auditorium with
John Markoff, who covers computers and technology for the New York
Times San Francisco. **Reprinted by permission of the New York
Times Electronic Media Company © 1997.**

7. Browse the Web

AOL supports web access. If you have been a long-time AOL
user (by today's standards, that means you've been a member
for more than two years), you have had the opportunity to
browse the web since early 1995, but you have had to do so
on a nonstandard browser that AOL supported exclusively for
several years.

Today, AOL versions 3.0 and later support the industry
standard browser, Netscape, as well as Microsoft's Internet

Explorer. If you would like to try using an industry-standard browser alongside AOL, you can download Netscape 3.0 by using the keyword *Netscape.*

Whether you use AOL's current built-in browser (Keyword: *Upgrade*, if you have a version of AOL prior to 3.0) or Netscape through AOL, you will be able to access and correctly display the majority of web pages you visit. Older web browsers might not support certain web features such as frames, tables, forms, and certain font type and color styles, for instance.

To access a web site, you will enter a web address, otherwise known as a URL. AOL provides three easy-access methods for viewing a web page: One way to access a web site on AOL is to double-click on a favorite place. Any time you bookmark a favorite place on the web, the address for that web page will be added to the Favorite Places window. Later, you can revisit your Favorite Places by pulling down the Go To menu and selecting Favorite Places. Simply double-click on the entry in the Favorite Places window for the place you'd like to revisit. (Macintosh users will find in Favorite Places an About AOL folder listing, where you can double-click entries such as AOL's Web Site.) All you have to do is double-click— the software will do the rest, including connecting to AOL if you were not already online.

A second way to access the web on AOL is to click on the Internet Connection channel. From there, you can enter a web address. If you want an activity to involve your audience, you might find useful material at the First Lines web site. By going to **http://pc159.lns.cornell.edu/firsts/**, you can test your recognition of the first lines of famous (and not so famous) books.

The third, and fastest, way to access any web site is to use the keyword screen and enter the full URL into the field.

Exercise

Use the keyword screen and access the ASTD web site, found at (**www.astd.org**). Read either the industry overview or about the seminars offered by satellite.

TECH TIP *It's not obvious, but you can have more than one web window open at once. All you have to do is enter another URL into the Keyword screen. When you are waiting for one web page to load or return results, open another web page to check out the latest humor, news, or business reports on another web site.*

TECH TIP *Once you are connected to AOL version 3.0 or later, you can launch another web browser if you like. For instance, you might prefer to work with the latest version of Netscape Navigator or Internet Explorer instead of the web browser included with AOL.*

TECH TIP **Create a Webliography**
One of the most useful ways to use your Internet connection for researching information is to create a "webliography,"* which is a listing of relevant, possibly annotated web sites that relate to a particular topic.

The general approach to creating your first webliography is to use the power of the search engines to show you what is available. Then you make several passes on the automated search results and enhance them using your professional judgment. The end result is a custom, hyperlinked page of relevant web sites that you can link to your web page or pass out to participants in a workshop.

* I believe I've coined the term *webliography* since I haven't seen it in print, but I could be mistaken. If you know of a prior usage, I'd appreciate your sending me e-mail at TechEdge_Update@BillRingle.com.

Here's how you start. Use your web browser to create the initial file of links. For the sake of simplicity, start with the browser not launched. Find your current bookmark file (book-marks.html) from the Preferences/Netscape/ directory and move it to a safe location on your hard drive. (If you are using Internet Explorer, do the same thing for your shortcuts file.)

Next, launch your web browser. You will now be starting from a blank slate for your bookmarks. Now go to various search engines, perform searches for sites that match your keywords, examine the results, visit the sites whose descriptions sound promising, and bookmark the ones that live up to their descriptions. Do this for a subject that matters to you and bookmark at least six sites before proceeding. Take notes either with a word processor/text editor open on your computer or just on a pad of paper on the side. Don't worry about the order in which you visit your sites, because that can be modified easily in the next step.

When you finish bookmarking at least half a dozen sites, you are ready to reorder the sites and then add the annotations. To reorganize the bookmarked sites, pull down the Window menu and select Bookmarks. You will see a window that looks like the one in Figure 5.5.

Here, you can drag the bookmarks up and down to position them as you like. In the example, let's say that the most important web site is the third one listed. Drag the third one to the top of the list. Make any other changes that you desire to your list, then quit Netscape to enable the bookmarks file to be edited by another application.

But first, a little housekeeping. Rename the bookmarks.html file. (Windows users may need to use .htm as the file name suffix in this example.) Call it researchNotes.html and move it to the root level of your hard drive so it is easy to find. Use your computer's operating system Find facility (either Find from the File menu in the

Figure 5.5

Bookmarks Window in Netscape Navigator

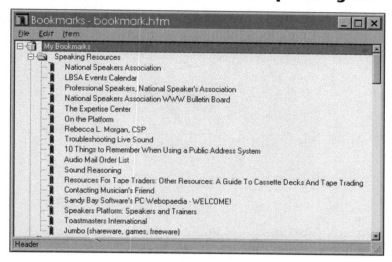

Copyright 1996 Netscape Communications Corp. Used with permission. All Rights Reserved. This electronic file or page may not be reprinted or copied without the express written permission of Netscape.

Macintosh Finder or Find from the Start menu of Windows 95) to locate a file called "bookmarks.html" or "bookmarks.htm."

Next, launch your favorite HTML editor, such as Claris Home Page, and open the researchNotes.html file. It will look something like the one in Figure 5.6.

Now type in the notes that go along with each site listed. The first two sites are annotated in Figure 5.7. You can embellish the page further by adding your logo and introductory information. Whether you plan to print and distribute the webliography or not, be sure to put your contact information at the bottom in case someone who reads your web page decides to print it and pass it along.

Figure 5.6

ResearchNotes.html before Annotation

Save your work and view it in Netscape. Test the links by clicking them to make sure they bring you to the expected site. Congratulations! That's your first webliography. Post it to your site and link it to the appropriate web pages.

Figure 5.7

ResearchNotes.html with Two Sites Annotated

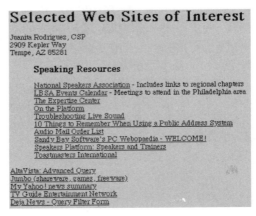

SUMMARY

How's that for some nitty-gritty? With the tips in Chapter 5, you've just gotten down and dirty with many of the important uses and features of America Online:

- How to obtain an AOL account
- How best to choose your screen name and set up other aspects of your online "identity"
- How to take advantage of the unique "online community" AOL provides—finding members with similar interests and establishing alternative online identities through screen names and profiles
- The basics of sending e-mail
- How to get help online from AOL's member service and support resources
- How to get free software, keep track of where you like to go online, and find information of interest to you
- How to use AOL as a jumping-off point to the Internet

Now that AOL has given you a taste of the larger Internet, you may be hungry for more! In Chapter 6, you'll learn about Internet Service Providers (ISPs).

 Define the following AOL-specific terms:
    screen name
    auditorium
    favorite place

Send an e-mail message containing an attached file to yourself (or to a friend on AOL). Learn how to use the Attach button in the Compose Mail window—try the online resources at keyword *help* if you're not sure how to do this.

Read some of the articles posted in AOL's Internet Connection channel to start your familiarization with the Internet, which we discuss in the next chapter.

6

ISP Services and What They Add

In order to get your telephone to work when you first plug it into the wall of a new house or office, you've got to let the local phone company know that you want service. When you call to make the arrangements (from a *working* telephone, of course!), what do you get? First, you get a number—a unique address that others on the phone network can dial to reach the telephone that sits on your desk. Second, you agree to pay the phone company for its services—typically a set-up fee and a monthly fee for maintaining the dial tone and network connections so that any time you pick up the phone, you can dial a number and reach virtually anyone in the world who has a phone.

The Internet is a lot like the telephone system, except that most people did not grow up with an "Internet dial tone" in their house. But follow the analogy: when you get an Internet service provider to connect your computer to the communications system, you want it to provide you with a way to reach others and them to reach you, as well as to take care of the technical details behind the scenes.

Unless you are involved in managing telephone services for a larger business, you probably do not spend a great deal of your time thinking about the different levels of telephone service. This is the world of trunk lines, PBXs, MANs, WANs, and LATA. In a similar way, Internet access has a lot of technical details behind it that are better left to explanations elsewhere. *The LAN Times Guide to Telephony* goes into more of the technical details for those who are interested.

For now, you need to be aware of two choices of how to access the Internet. Do you want to have access through a commercial online service like AOL, or do you want direct access through an Internet service provider?

Without a doubt, connecting to the Internet through an ISP is harder than going through AOL. You have additional communications software to configure, which is generally not as user-friendly as a COS installation kit. If you are installing an ISP kit after working with AOL, you risk deinstalling the AOL configuration settings. Once you get on the Internet, you don't have the helpful interface that helps you navigate through the online content; you don't have access to the AOL reference, support, and file library areas; and you are paying about the same monthly fee of $20, which does not include any nonlocal telephone charges.

WHAT IS AN ISP?

An Internet service provider (ISP) is a business that provides Internet access and services. ISPs can be local, regional, or national. Some of the most experienced, larger, and better-known ISPs are Alternet, PSInet, UUnet, and BBN. In addition, the long-distance phone companies have decided that this is a business in which they are interested, so think of AT&T, Sprint, and MCI as ISPs as well.

So why bother signing up with an Internet service provider? Here are a few good reasons.

1. You want access more of the time. You might live in an area that has a lot of competition for the available modem lines during the times when you most need to get online. Or you have been frustrated by the notice saying that a particular AOL area or data source is currently

unavailable, which is perhaps more annoying than being unable to get phone access. Once connected, you have a right to expect that AOL's advertised, regular services are available.

2. You want to avoid additional phone charges. Perhaps AOL doesn't have a local number in your area and the 800 number is becoming too costly to use on a regular basis. If an ISP has a dial-up location in your local calling area, you could save money on your connection time and still access AOL content and services through your ISP.

3. You want to use Internet tools that are not supported by AOL. AOL's e-mail tool is weak in a number of significant areas, such as custom mail boxes for sorting mail; automatic mail actions based on mail header information such as the sender, the subject, and the time of day; and more flexible ways to sort and manage mail. For higher-volume mail traffic or more sophisticated business purposes, Eudora and Claris Emailer are far superior. These software applications, discussed in the following two chapters, cannot be used with an AOL connection alone—an ISP connection is required.

4. You are dissatisfied with your present access provider. Customer service is crucial, especially in industries in which consumers have many choices from which to purchase services. Internet access falls into this category. If you have had problems with an online service provider that have not been resolved to your satisfaction; if some company has insulted a friend, associate, or even a writer you like; if a new release of its software leaves you feeling underwhelmed; if a particular company has not served you well due to incompetence or insensitivity, then you have the right and ability to take your business elsewhere.

5. Your business image would be enhanced by a well-planned, unified Internet presence. A positive reason for adding ISP services is to register a domain name related to your business and provide information to other business people on the Internet.

Your business has the ability to be represented on the Internet on a par with every other organization. A business of one can have as large and as impressive a site on the Internet as a Fortune 500 multinational company. The Internet levels the playing field in this respect.

When striving to convey a professional image, do not sabotage your efforts by presenting multiple fronts. It is confusing to see two or more e-mail addresses on a business card. How is someone to know which is your primary, or preferred, address? Another example is having a web site at **www.mynewwebsite.com** and then listing your e-mail address in totally different terms, such as Pat@localCollege.edu or some other address. If you go to the trouble of obtaining your own domain name, be sure to find an ISP that will fully implement your web site and e-mail needs.

WHY SHOULD A SPEAKER, TRAINER, OR CONSULTANT NEED TO MAKE A CHOICE?

Beyond the "walls" of a commercial online service is a vast network of people sharing information, job leads, and the latest and greatest about many areas that affect your business. You can reach much of this information from an online service, but unless the service supports a full dial-up connection, you will be restricted in the software you can use to access that other information.

For example, CompuServe, Prodigy, and older versions of AOL force you to use their web browsers. It was intended to be convenient because the web browser was linked with their online access software. However, it was ineffective because the software they used was inferior to the more sophisticated Netscape Navigator and Internet Explorer and you could not use alternative browsers through their connections. Also, since the browser software was a separate application, it launched separately and took up more system memory to operate. This created a challenging situation for users running computers with less than 16 MB of RAM.

Fortunately, AOL 3.0 creates a standard PPP connection when you dial up. This means that once you are connected, you can launch any browser you wish, and it will connect to the Internet through the dial-up connection.

HOW DO ISP COMPANIES OPERATE?

The ISP company operates the most fragile and most customer-service-intensive end of a long string of network connections: the incoming modem connection from end-users of network services. Like the airlines, Internet service providers oversell their capacity on the assumption that not all of their customers want to access the Internet at the exact same time. This planning leads to stress on both the equipment and the customers, which is alleviated by adding more modems to keep the ratio of users to modems within industry standards. Once more modems are installed, access to the ISP becomes easier because the traffic bottleneck has been loosened. Meanwhile, the marketing department sends out more brochures to increase the number of customers. As more customers sign up, the see-saw swings back toward the direction of tighter access until management decides to purchase more modems. This same scenario takes place with commercial online service providers, but, in general, they have greater financial and technical resources than many ISPs.

Another fundamental part of an ISP's business is selling dedicated line connections to businesses that require local area network (LAN) connectivity, such as schools, banks, insurance offices, magazine publishers, research firms, and other companies. While a dedicated connection can cost from several hundred dollars to several thousand dollars a month, the major advantage is that the connection is always present. Modems are unnecessary. When an office computer is always connected to the Internet, a company has a great deal more flexibility in determining the kinds of services they can offer their customers and the kind of expanded presence they can have on the Internet. While extremely interesting to organizations ready to make the commitment to support them, dedicated connections are of little interest to most speakers, trainers, and consultants.

WHAT DOES IT COST?

Basic dial-up access to an ISP should cost between $20 and $30 monthly, depending on where you live. The closer you are to a metropolitan area, the more likely competition will keep the costs around $20 per month. Beware of "specials" offering "unlimited" access for less than this amount. Because of the cost of a basic telephone connection, ISPs cannot sustain a business by charging customers less than $20 monthly and still maintain equipment, pay their sales and technical support staffs, and earn enough profit to be able to stay in business. An ISP that charges less than $20 monthly either says it is for a limited number of hours or faces one of two futures: (1) It will raise its charges after a given time, and, if you wish to avoid moving to another ISP, you will have to pay the new rate; or (2) the ISP will go out of business and you will have to move your access to another ISP anyway.

SUMMARY

When you've outgrown what a commercial online service like AOL has to offer, ISPs are a good choice for further Internet exploration. As you've learned, opening an account with an Internet service provider is a good choice for you

■ when access problems cause trouble with AOL,

■ when you need additional capabilities not offered by a COS, or

■ when having an Internet presence can contribute to your business image.

Chapter 6 has given you a basic understanding of what ISPs offer, how they operate, and how much service costs. If you're ready to move to a different type of connection to the online world, Chapter 7 points out what's important to keep in mind when choosing an Internet service provider.

If you subscribe to a COS, look at the time you've spent online for the past three months. Find the average and see if it exceeds 20 hours per month.

Factors to Consider When Selecting an ISP

HOW TO LOCATE THEM IN YOUR AREA

ISPs operate independently from each other, and you won't find a national umbrella organization that lists them. So, here are a few suggestions on how to locate the group of ISPs nearest you.

Many people would turn to the yellow pages, but outside of Silicon Valley in California, Silicon Alley in New York City, and Multimedia Gulch in Austin, Texas, the telephone companies have been very slow to recognize the Internet sector. Look for this to change as AT&T, MCI, and Sprint take over a larger share of the business.

At the end of this section, you'll read a checklist for questions to ask when considering an ISP. Right now, let's get started with a few ways of locating these businesses.

Let's start with the simplest, least expensive, most direct methods which require no Internet access and proceed from there. First, look in the newspaper. In the business section of every metropolitan newspaper, you will find a small but growing section of Internet service providers listing their services. If you don't find listings in the daily papers, be sure to look in the Sunday edition. Some of the ads will be larger than others, but bigger doesn't always mean better—it just means they decided to spend more money on their advertisements.

Second, check out the local user groups. User Groups are the single best investment of your time for keeping up on your hardware and software needs. Typically, this nonprofit group of volunteers meets monthly to swap stories, tips, techniques, and insights. Membership fees are usually in the range of $25 to $100 annually and pay for monthly meetings, a newsletter full of tips and conference reports, access to shareware libraries, and possibly a web site with additional members-only information. Having participated in user group meetings and presented to them over the years, I strongly recommend joining regardless of your level of understanding and experience. You will find people there who know much more than you who are willing to lend you a hand, as well as those who will be able to benefit from the lessons you've learned. You can reach the User Group Connection at (408) 477-4277 or online at **www.ugconnection.com** to locate the nearest Mac or PC user group in your area. If you have an Internet connection, you can also view a list of User groups at **www.yahoo.com/Computers_and_Internet/Per sonal_Computers/**. At any user group meeting, you can ask members about their personal experiences connecting to ISPs.

Third, browse the Yahoo! collection of pointers to ISPs on the web. Once online, you can shop around for competitive services. Even if you are not online, you can ask a friend to help you research an ISP. Yahoo! has an extensive list of ISPs that are listed under **www.yahoo.com/Business_and_ Economy/Companies/Internet_Services/Internet_ Access_Providers/Directories/**. For example, if you want to find all the ISPs that offer toll-free support lines, you can visit **www.celestin.com/pocia/cgi/search.pl?what=area&s earchstring=800**. More are added all the time, so you might want to see what's offered before going to The List.

Fourth, go to The List (**thelist.iworld.com**). At publication, this web site, provided by Mecklermedia, had about 4,500 ISPs internationally and provided look-up capabilities by state as well as by zip code. The List is one of the first services to consolidate ISP listings around the country. It has helped to get businesses of all sizes online by giving them a well-organized source of useful information. The List provides the name, phone, and fax of each ISP; the area codes it serves; and pricing information on the services offered (dial-up speeds, dedicated connection costs, services in addition to e-mail and Internet access offered, etc.).

Fifth, participate in a college course—day, evening, or weekend—on any subject. "Whoa—isn't that a big overhead cost just to find out about ISPs?" you may ask. Actually, you will gain a lot of value by signing up for a course at a local college. Consider the following benefits:

1. With your library privileges, you get Internet access on a very fast connection, using college-owned computers. If you need to take files back to your office, you can transfer them to a diskette.
2. You also may get access to trained technical support. Universities generally have consultants and trainers to support academic computing efforts. They are very familiar with the hardware, networks, and beginners' common problems and are available for drop-in or call-in questions.
3. It's actually an income-generating opportunity for you. Remember, the recommendation was to "participate" in a college course, which can mean as a potential instructor in your own field in that college. Even if you have no interest in teaching and simply sign up for a course, you can use the class to network with other business professionals, make contact with faculty members in your areas of expertise, exchange ideas, and incorporate what you learn from the course to update your materials.

QUESTIONS TO ASK WHEN SELECTING AN ISP

Does It Provide Software?

The better ISPs have figured out that by providing new customers with connection software and a few Internet applications up front, they save enormous costs down the road with support questions. The first reason you need special software is to create the PPP connection to the Internet. PPP stands for Point-to-Point Protocol, and it simply means you are using the TCP/IP network protocol over a modem connection so you can access Internet services. If the ISP provides the software, configured so that your modem dials up its modem bank and logs in successfully to its network, it has done both itself and its customers a big favor. The larger ISPs, such as Sprint, AT&T, PSI, and BBNPlanet, all offer this type of software package. If the ISP you are talking to does not offer this type of connection software and you are not experienced or interested in learning how to debug modem connection strings, move on to the next ISP on your list.

When considering a potential ISP, ask about (or look on its web site for) connection software; PPP dialers; or information for configuring MacTCP (for Mac), Trumpet Winsock (for Windows 3.1), or Windows Dial-Up Networking (for Windows 95/97/NT). If this information is not discussed, or if there is not a connection software package offered by the ISP, you may have difficulty using this ISP's services.

The second reason an ISP should provide Internet software is to give you the most benefit from its service. By providing an e-mail package, a web browser, a news reader, an FTP client, and various utilities for decoding multimedia and compressed files, it is saving the new Internet user a great deal of time in getting ready to perform useful work on the Net.

Since e-mail is the most critical tool for speakers, trainers, and consultants, consider this recommendation carefully. If you use both AOL and an ISP and you want to keep things simple, you couldn't get a better program than Claris Emailer [Claris Corporation, (800) 325-2747, **www.claris.com**]. In a single communications application, you have the ability to send, receive, and file mail from your AOL, ISP, CompuServe, Prodigy, and Claris Office Mail and Radio Mail accounts.

A very flexible and powerful program is Eudora [Qual-comm, 800-238-3672, **www.eudora.com**], recommended for business professionals who just need to access mail from an ISP account. Eudora's spelling checker, custom mailboxes, hot links to URLs, and automated filters make it a favorite among business professionals, sales associates, and telecom-muters as well as speakers, trainers, and consultants who rely on e-mail.

If your ISP provides connection software, but not the application software, don't despair! Rather than try to assemble all the parts and pieces yourself, you can buy a software toolkit of public domain and shareware software for $40 or less. *The Internet Starter Kit,* by Adam Engst, is famous for providing the best explanations as well as the best collections of software. Both Mac and Windows editions are available in national bookstores such as Borders or Barnes & Noble.

Is the ISP's Service Available via a Local Call from Your Exchange?

Depending on where you live, you may find few or many ISPs in your area. Remember, just because an ISP offers dial-up service to your area code, it doesn't mean the calls are free! Be aware of what costs are associated with a call to a particular exchange. It may seem inconsequential now, but when your first monthly phone bill comes, you will be better prepared if you know the charges in advance.

You can use this information either to disqualify an ISP as a likely candidate or to readjust the definition of a local call by contacting your local phone company. By paying a higher monthly rate of a few dollars, you might be able to save yourself hundreds of dollars annually depending on your use of the dial-up connection.

What Type of Connection Does the ISP Have to the Internet?

The primary service an ISP delivers is access to the Internet. At one end of its business, it has customers dialing in and connecting to its network at modem speeds of 14.4 or 28.8 KB/s. At the other end, it has a high-speed connection to another part of the Internet. What most customers don't realize is that the speed of an ISP's connection can vary widely. What most customers do realize when their connections are terribly slow is that something is terribly wrong. If you imagine a traffic jam going over a bridge during rush hour, you begin to get the idea about network resource constraints. How can you tell in advance whether this is a likely scenario with your ISP?

Here's how: use simple division to determine its peak capacity. Find out the size of the ISP's outgoing trunk line (T1 circuits can carry up to 1.54 MB/s; T3 circuits can handle triple that capacity at 45 MB/s). Most ISPs have one or more T1 lines. Then divide the outbound capacity by the inbound modem pool speed.

For example, if an ISP has a single T1 and has all 28.8 KB/s modems, they can have up to 536 modems active at one time under ideal conditions, and assuming the trunk line is fully dedicated to customers. Scale that back by 10 percent to account for in-house use and real-world line stressors and your ISP under these conditions should have no more than

480 28.8 KB/s modems. A modem rack of 500 wouldn't bother me. A rack of 2000 on a single T1 would.

An ISP's ability to serve its customers is based on the bandwidth of its connection. Smart and ethical ISPs will use this same capacity calculation as a planning benchmark and build in additional bandwidth as customer demand warrants.

What Is the Modem/Pool Ratio?

Another industry standard measurement is the ratio of users to modems. An acceptable range is 20:1. A smaller number indicates a better chance of getting connected during peak usage. The higher the ratio, the better the chance of getting a busy signal when you want to connect.

Does It Provide Adequate Support Hours/ Equipment/Staff?

Are you a user who relies on a friendly, knowledgeable voice on the other end of a phone to help you through a technical snafu? If so, you should call the tech support department and ask a question before you sign up. Notice the kind of response you get and whether it instills confidence in the ISP's service department.

In addition, it is fair game to ask the support department what kind of computers they are using. If they have something similar to what you have on your desk, the chances are better that they have encountered your difficulty before and have solved it or can easily reproduce the problem and get to the solution.

Another litmus test for ISP service departments is to leave a voice message and see what happens. Do you get a call back? Does the technician have an answer or proposed solution to try out when he or she calls? Do you get the sense that your satisfaction is important, or is the technician simply putting a check mark in the Status Closed column?

What Does Web Space Cost? How Much Do You Get?

On a commercial online service provider, you can set up a web page for no additional cost. AOL customers can use up to 2 MB of hard drive space on AOL host computers for the basic account, which on publication was about $20 monthly for unlimited use.

Since you are being charged an additional amount, you have to weigh that against what the ISP will provide you. Your ISP can provide you with a custom domain name, which is a value-added service. Your ISP can also allow you to use more than 2 MB of disk space for an additional fee. Savvy AOL customers will note that while AOL allows 2 MB of disk space per account name and 5 account names per billing, clever URL linking can produce 10 MB of space.

How Long Has the ISP Been in Business?

You want to understand the risks of signing on with an ISP that has been in business less than a year. With the large long-distance carriers operating in this space now, the little "ISP from a garage" operations may experience significant challenges to their revenue streams.

If your ISP was forced out of business next week, what would be the impact on your business? Would your e-mail from important clients be forwarded to your new account? Would hits to your web pages be transparently redirected? The answer under real-world conditions are hard to predict, but the service contract should spell out what measures the company will take to protect your online access/presence in advance.

Are There Any Savings for Prepayment Plans?

Some ISPs offer discounts for annual prepayments instead of monthly charges. These payments help reduce their overhead and they pass the savings along to the customer. Find out if this option is available.

What Do You Get for Your Monthly Fee?
Set-Up/Activation Fee?

Ask for a list of services and the additional charge associated with each. The $20 monthly charge probably provides only dial-up access.

Will the ISP Grow with Your Business?
Any Limitations?

Find out before you sign up with an ISP what its plans are for expansion over the next 12 to 24 months. What new markets will it be pursuing? What new services will it be offering its customers?

In the next few years, ISP services will become more and more a commodity item. How will your ISP strive to differentiate itself, add value for its customers, and grow to survive?

EVALUATING THE DECISION TO
CONNECT THROUGH COS VERSUS ISP

Some of the critical issues to consider as a speaker are the amount of time you have available to learn and master a new service, how much you travel, whether you have support help back at your office, and what your sources of help are when you run into a complication or have a tough question.

SUMMARY

If you've decided that an ISP is right for you, now you know how to make the right selection using the information in Chapter 7.

- How to find ISPs, either large national companies or smaller firms in your area, that you can access via a local call
- How to select the billing options that are right for your budget
- How to find out what software is provided so you'll know which software you'll have to get on your own
- How to find out how well the ISP connects to the Internet—the speed of its connection and the breadth of its modem pool
- How to evaluate an ISP's customer service, technical support, costs for additional service options, and long-term potential (will it stay in business, and can it grow with you?)

You've made your ISP choice; now you're ready to start using the wide variety of powerful services available through your provider. Chapter 8 will get you started.

 Contact a computer user group in your area. Think of one specific area of using your computer that you would like to learn more about. Attend a meeting and ask for help. What did you learn?

Make a list of three ISPs in your local calling area. Visit their web sites, and call them to ask about their services and resources as suggested in this chapter.

How much information was posted on their web sites? Were the sites easy to use? Could you find information and support contacts easily? During your phone calls, how were your questions responded to by the salespeople? Finally, ask yourself: Is this a company that you would like to depend on for services?

What You Can Do on the Internet

Having Internet access through an ISP means having great flexibility in terms of the software you use, such as e-mail and web browsers. In this chapter, you will learn how to expand your use of these tools to help you connect with valuable information resources.

SEVEN ESSENTIAL FEATURES FOR YOUR INTERNET E-MAIL

As mentioned in Chapter 7, many ISPs provide software in a sign-up kit. Some software kits come on a floppy disk and contain fairly simple communications software that can be configured for an ISP's dial-up service. Other software kits are more extensive, arriving on a CD that contains dozens of public domain software applications and information files for learning, working, communicating, and playing on the Internet. Having this additional software makes using the Internet through an ISP both more interesting and more challenging than through a commercial online service such as AOL.

Internet mail, by definition, uses SMTP (Simple Mail Transfer Protocol) mail servers to send mail and the POP (Post Office Protocol) mail servers to receive mail. When you send mail, your e-mail client software needs to reach an SMTP mail server, which passes the message along to the POP mail server. When you check for messages, your e-mail client contacts the POP mail server and requests to be sent a copy of any messages that have accumulated in your account mailbox.

Two of the most popular e-mail client packages for SOHOs (Small Office Home Offices) are Eudora by Qualcomm and Claris Emailer. Both give you a great deal of flexibility and power. They are affordable (Eudora and Emailer each cost about $60) and have easy-to-learn interfaces.

Internet e-mail packages have the same capabilities as the AOL software for creating, sending, and receiving messages and attaching files but extend these capabilities and add new features to make them distinctive. The following features should be on your list when evaluating a software package for your business and personal needs.

1. Nickname Capabilities

E-mail nicknames allow you to type an abbreviated or informal name on an address line and have it translated by the e-mail application when the message is sent. Nicknames are a form of shorthand. For instance, you may correspond with three people whose first name is John. Rather than type out each John's name and e-mail address each time you wish to send mail to one of them, you can simply type a nickname such as JohnSmith or BigJohn or John from Maine on the address line. Just before sending the mail, the actual e-mail address is substituted for the nickname. So, BigJohn might be switched to John_Edwards@BigNet.com, and you didn't have to remember or type the longer name once it was set up the first time.

Nicknames also allow you to create group addresses easily. You can create a nickname for "Family" and send out announcements and messages to your relatives who have e-mail addresses.

Figure 8.1

Eudora Nicknames Screen

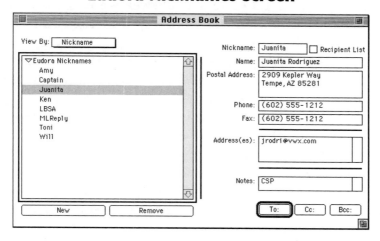

You can add or modify nicknames quite easily. Nicknames are usually stored in a file that is accessible through the e-mail program you are using. In Eudora, the nicknames interface looks like that shown in Figure 8.1.

When you add a nickname, you are prompted by the software to provide a nickname and the actual address or addresses that correspond to that nickname. What can make nickname discussions a bit confusing is that the term *nickname* refers both to the abbreviated form of the e-mail address and to the set of information containing the abbreviated address and actual address.

After saving a nickname, you can modify either the short address, such as BigJohn, or the actual address in the event that John moves his account to another ISP.

2. Having a Full Range of Responses to Mail

When you start to get more than a dozen pieces of mail each day due to gregarious friends, follow-up work from seminars, or active mailing lists, you will appreciate the ability to sort through your mail and act accordingly. As with office paper work, you want to read mail and decide whether to delegate, delete, or archive each message.

Nearly every e-mail package allows you to reply and forward mail simply by issuing a keyboard command or clicking an icon. When you get a message announcing a conference to which you would like to present, you will respond to that announcement, making sure that the address line contains the organizer's e-mail address and not the person (or mail list) who passed along the information!

Deleting mail is very useful. Make every effort to keep the number of messages in your primary "In" mail box as low as possible. Many mail messages don't deserve to be read more than once. If you get a message from a friend confirming a lunch appointment, you jot the information down in your PDA or day planner and delete the message.

The ability to help you sort messages that are important enough to keep is really the strength of programs like Eudora and Emailer. In these programs, you can create mailboxes as easily as you create folders to sort files on your hard drive. If you begin project discussions with the VP of human resources at Prudential Insurance, for example, you can create a new mail box called Prudential Project and file all mail that you send or receive regarding this opportunity in this location.

3. Automated Filters/Actions

Having a place to sort your mail so you can easily find it again is a useful thing. Having an e-mail program with the ability to put mail into those folders for you is a very useful thing!

This capability is known as mail filtering. In Eudora, the feature is called automated filters; on Emailer, it is called actions. Here's how it works.

Think of a mail filter like a coin sorter at a bank or casino. A bunch of coins are tossed into a hopper that jiggles the coins and sends them rolling down a chute. Depending on each coin's size, it drops into a slot for dimes, pennies, nickels, or quarters. The slot leads to a tube of the correct size for the anticipated coin, helping to organize and count the coins. A mail filter likewise takes groups of e-mail messages and reads information in the header and body to determine the sender, the recipient, the subject, and the content. Then it compares this information against filter rules that instruct it to perform actions such as:

- When mail from joe.jones@ibm.com arrives, put it in the IBM_JoeJones mailbox.
- Move any mail message that contains the phrase "be sure to send a copy of this message to 10 friends," from the In Box to the trash.
- If a message arrives that contains the phrase "driving directions" in the subject line, open the message window and print this message to my local printer.

Eudora 3.0 allows you to assign up to 5 actions (any of 15 action commands, such as play a sound, move to a mailbox, or automatically reply) to each filter rule.

4. Hot Internet Addresses

Often, you will get an e-mail message from someone who recommends that you visit a web site. The URL is included in the message, and simply by double-clicking on the URL, the e-mail program launches your web browser, sends it the web address, and displays the site.

The three most common types of hot addresses you will encounter are:

- Web addresses: "Look at **<http://www.internet-mall.com/>**, they're accepting orders for snack delivery!"
- FTP addresses: "You can get the latest FAQ for this new group at **<ftp://rtfm.mit.edu>**."
- E-mail: "Please keep my materials on file in case a need for my services opens up in the near future. You can reach me fastest through my e-mail account: **<mailto:hank@ConsultantsRUs.com>**."

Two aspects of the format of these hot links bear mention. First, the angle brackets are optional and only serve to increase readability. When an Internet address is enclosed in the angle brackets on an e-mail system that supports hot addresses, the address is usually highlighted in blue like a hot link in a web browser, and the angle brackets are not highlighted. In e-mail packages that don't have the hot address feature, the angle brackets set the address apart from the rest of the text and help identify the address for the reader to highlight with the mouse, copy, and paste into the appropriate field in his or her web browser (for a web or ftp address) or a mail message (for an e-mail address).

Second, the e-mail address needs to have the standard Internet service prefix attached in order to be recognized as a hot address. For example, the address **www.internet-mall.com** can be pasted into the location field of Netscape and be displayed with or without the **http://** services prefix. However, without the services prefix, the address would not be properly recognized in a mail program.

5. Attachments to E-Mail Messages

Computer files such as spreadsheet budgets, word processing proposals, or even publicity pictures can be sent along with e-mail messages, the same way that a large postal envelope can hold both a cover letter and enclosures.

When mail message enclosures are sent within a computer system, from one ISP account to another account in the same ISP—for instance, from Joe@EarthLink.com to Paul@Earth-Link.com—the mail enclosure has an easy time following the e-mail message. When an enclosure is sent to any other mail host (from an EarthLink to an AOL account, for example), the transfer becomes a bit trickier, literally. These "enclosures" are known in the Internet world as attachments.

SMTP and POP mail servers operate by exchanging text files, which are represented as 7-bits per character. Binary files, which include specially formatted characters as well as program files, are represented as 8-bits per character formats. In order to send a binary file across SMTP and POP servers, the content of the file must be temporarily translated, or encoded, as a 7-bit format prior to sending and then decoded once it is received.

Several standards for performing this translation have been adopted over the years. UUencoding originated on the Unix platform. BinHex is the Macintosh equivalent. MIME (Multipart Internet Mail Exchange) is the most recently developed and widely used standard system for performing this translation process.

MIME encoding allows you to send files as message attachments across the Internet. These file attachments are not limited in size by MIME or the mail servers, though your

ISP may limit the size of files it allows across its network. AOL, for example, allows files only up to 1 MB in size to be sent to Internet addresses outside its system; internal attachments must be less than 16 MB. Another benefit of MIME enclosures is that this method works with files of any type. While word processing files are typically less than 20 K in size, graphics files can easily grow to 10 MB. Once you start to add audio and movie clips to a presentation, it can easily grow in size beyond 20 MB or even 100 MB.

MIME is implemented at the client end, which is both good news and bad news. The good news is that you are generally not at the mercy of your ISP to take advantage of MIME encoding. If your e-mail client supports MIME, you can send and receive MIME attachments. Versions of Eudora 1.x and Emailer 2.x and later support MIME. But what about if you or the person you are exchanging mail with use a non-MIME client? That's the bad news. The text e-mail message will come across fine, but the attached file will likely arrive in an unusable format.

MIME is so widely used that if you have purchased an e-mail package in the last year or two, it should support this standard. One of the greatest benefits of MIME is the ability to exchange files with colleagues, clients, and suppliers around the world in a way that transports the files quickly and reliably and is platform independent. So, if you send a slide show created on the Macintosh version of PowerPoint as an e-mail attachment to a corporate contact, that person could use a Windows version of PowerPoint to read, display, and print the presentation. Internet mail puts the file on the recipient's hard drive, and using the file is simply a matter of opening it with a compatible application.

 When sending attachments, be sure to let the recipient know what application you used to create it. A

simple note such as "Enclosed is my proposal, which was writ-ten in Word 6.0" lets the recipient know what application is needed to open the file.

Compression Software

Compression methods are useful in reducing the size of files prior to sending them. One benefit of compressed files is the decrease in the time it takes to send and receive an attached file. Another advantage of using compression is the ability to send a group of files together as a single e-mail enclosure.

When you are sending parcels across the Internet, com-pression software performs both the vacuum packing and boxing functions. At the sending end, you have to be con-cerned with compressing and encoding the files; with files that you receive, you need to be able to decode and uncom-press the files you download. The compression process makes the file smaller for faster transmission. The encoding/decod-ing process makes sure that the file arrives at its destination intact.

AOL software has these functions built in, as does Claris Emailer. AOL has the Stuffit engine incorporated into its client software to assist with these functions for its mail attachments as well as for file downloads from the software library.

If you are using an ISP account, the ISP will typically include this type of software in the start-up kit. Aladdin's Stuffit is a widely used, cross-platform compression/decompres-sion package. At its web site (**www.aladdinsys.com**), you can download the uncompression software (called Unstuffit) as free shareware for either the PC or Macintosh. WinZip and PK-Zip are the well-known, but older, packages on the PC side.

6. Defining Your Signature

Reading through your in box, you see three new messages. At the bottom of the first message you see:

```
John Jones, Strategic Planning Expert        JJones@xyz.com
"Your Future is Our Business"                212-555-1212  v
Website: http://www.strategic-planning.xyz.com  212-555-2323  f
```

At the bottom of the second message appears:

```
Patricia Anderson
PatSpeaks@wxy.com
Contact Pat to motivate and energize your next sales meeting.
Phone: 313-555-1212    Fax: 313-555-2222
Mail: 1001 Powell Road  •  Little Falls, NY 12111
```

Following the third message, you see:

```
\\\|||///  \ Bill Roy, CSP
\\ ~ ~ //   \ mailto:bilroy@uvw.com
 | @ @ |     \ www: http://www.uvw.com/~bilroywashere/
oOo (_) oOo   \ "Bilroy was here"
```

E-mail signatures are not necessary to identify who sent the mail. That information is contained in the "From" line of the mail header. Consider the following three purposes for e-mail signatures:

1. To introduce or identify the context of the sender's message
2. To provide pertinent information beyond what is contained in the mail
3. To share a personal philosophy, Meyers-Briggs type, opinion, or witticism

Eudora and Emailer support signatures. Eudora even allows you to create multiple signatures and select the appro-

priate one for a particular message. You may want one for
business, one for friends, one for family, one for each of the
associations you belong to if you hold a leadership position.
Follow these guidelines:

- Keep your signature brief—four lines or less.
- Use the appropriate context, whether business, family,
  volunteer organization, or other.
- Avoid silly pictures. They are amusing, but not always
  appropriate. You might want to save some choice footer
  pictures in a file for special occasions. Check the book's
  web site (**techedge.BillRingle.com**) for some examples
  to stimulate your thinking.
- Keep it up to date. Because footers are not shown in your
  mail until the time it is sent, it is not something that you
  are likely to notice without conscious effort.
- Check to see how it arrives in your mail. Sometimes spac-
  ing and special characters can be altered as it is sent
  through different mail systems. A good way to keep your
  footers up to date and properly formatted is to send yourself a piece of test mail and read it. Another way is to cc
  your e-mail address when sending mail to someone else
  and see how it comes through. A third way to check is to
  send someone mail and ask them how the footer looks.
  This last method might be necessary if you suspect that a
  particular mail server is affecting the characters used in
  your e-mail.

7. Directory Information

A directory is a place to look up information on a group of
people. Your local phone directory will give you the phone
number of a person whose name you provide if he or she is
listed in that directory. An online directory is a database that
can be searched. Generally, it provides e-mail address information for people who are listed.

For AOL, CompuServe, and other commercial online services, this model makes sense because members want to find
out about other members—particularly through the member
profile listings. ISPs do not generally maintain or make available this kind of customer information. Aside from the COSs,
look for online directories wherever you have a community
of people learning, working, or having fun together online.
Corporations and universities are common places to find
directories, and Eudora allows you to access this information
without having to leave the program. Simply by entering the
address of a directory into the Directory Services area and
supplying a name to look up, Eudora will send a query to the
online directory and display whatever results it finds.

E-mail directories on the web, such as Four11 (**www.four
11.com**), are useful for locating people who could be on any
Internet ISP. In the future, you can expect these web-based
directories to become integrated with your e-mail application's
built-in address book (Microsoft's Internet Mail for Windows
already offers this feature).

JOIN AN INTERNET MAIL LIST

A list server (also known as a "listserver" or sometimes "list-
serv" when the host is restricted to eight-character file
names), is a name for an Internet mail list. To be precise, a list
server is the name of the software that manages the mailing
list functions, such as allowing people to subscribe and
unsubscribe themselves. List servers are applications that run
on a server, which is a computer dedicated to performing
client–server transactions.

In general, a mailing list is a way to make sure that all the
people who are interested in a certain topic receive messages
from others who are exploring and learning about that topic
via e-mail. On the Internet, membership with public list
servers are available at no charge to the members. For

instance, all consultants who work on helping companies develop mission statements, work processes, and strategies would belong to an organizational development mailing list. A university might be the sponsor of such a list if this was an area of interest to the management department.

Usually, a list server is an ongoing exchange, and there are several different ways to participate in a list. Some lists are open to all, some have membership open only by invitation. Your alternatives with public lists are unmoderated and moderated lists (private lists operate the same way, except that you have to be invited to join).

Unmoderated lists allow any member to send messages out to all other members. The mail is sent to the group as it is received by the mail list server. This is one of the most popular ways to run a list server, since it gives participants the most freedom to contribute as much and as frequently as each wishes. This arrangement works best when the group is experienced with list server culture and etiquette. Like a clique at a cocktail party, each list has a personality based upon the participants and flavored by the theme of what brought the group together. A group of research scientists discussing organic pigmentation methods has a different tone to its discussion than does a group of trainers recounting the funniest group responses to active listening exercises. More important than the theme is the experience level of the group, because unmoderated groups are largely self-policing when people get off topic.

For instance, both groups just mentioned would be rightfully upset if someone used the mailing list address to advertise a car for sale. Solicitation of any kind on mailing lists is considered bad form and the contributor who went out of bounds would be chastised for the transgression, politely for the first offense. Repeated postings that violate or ignore the intention of a mailing list can result in warnings and ultimately in removal from a list. But who among the dozens, hundreds, or even thousands of members would be called upon to take this action? The list master, of course!

Though designated as unmoderated, each mail list has someone who is ultimately responsible for its operation. This person is usually the one who operates the list server software, but it could also be someone designated by the group. This person is called the List Master, Listmeister, or List Mom, and someone of either gender can claim any appellation that she or he chooses.

When a group is new to the Internet, the topic is likely to generate many redundant and/or controversial postings. If membership is by invitation only, the structure of a list is more appropriately moderated than unmoderated.

Moderated lists require that all submissions be sent to an individual address rather than simply blasted out to all the members by the list server software. This individual, the moderator, makes editorial decisions as to which messages are sent out to the group and which are redundant or off the stated topic. The moderator then forwards the appropriate ones to the list server to distribute to the group. In essence, an unmoderated list operates exactly like a moderated list, except that the moderator is the only member who is allowed to send to the address that forwards the mail to the group.

Organizations will sometimes sponsor a list server to promote communication among professionals across different geographies or industries. It is quite common in the technology industry for a company to sponsor a support mailing list for its products. It is not unusual for a company that has the capabilities to sponsor a list for another company or organization as a for-profit service or in exchange for advertising rights or other business favors of comparable worth.

For instance, StarComm sponsors private Internet mailing lists on a barter arrangement for several association chapter officers, which allows only those individuals to post and receive messages. It is a win–win situation for the nonprofit organizations who cannot afford the overhead of maintaining a list. The economies of scale allow StarComm to perform the services quite routinely, and many times the association members are clients/potential clients of StarComm's Internet consulting, training, or development business.

How to Join an Internet List

The vehicle for mailing lists is e-mail. When you know how to send a message to someone by putting the address into the "To:" field of the message window, filling in the subject field, then writing a message in the body, you know the essential skills for using Internet mail lists.

As a reader of this book, you are invited to join the TechEdge mailing list. Simply send e-mail addressed to TechEdge@BillRingle.com. Put the word `subscribe techedge` and your first and last name in the body of the message. Send the message and you will be on a list of TechEdge subscribers. A welcome message will be returned to you. Read the welcome message carefully for late-breaking news and special instructions.

There is no charge to participate in this mailing list. It is an unmoderated list for TechEdge readers who want to continue to share ideas, tips, and techniques on the topics in the book.

Where to Find Out More

Here are three places to look to find more information about public mailing lists.

1. The easiest place to look is at your local bookstore. Racks and racks of Internet books are filled with web sites and mailing list locations. Look for books with titles such as *Internet Yellow Pages*.

2. Use AOL's searchable database of mailing lists in the Internet Connection channel, or at keyword *mailing lists.*

3. Use a web-based directory of Internet mailing lists, such as Liszt (**www.liszt.com**) or Inter-Links (**www.nova.edu/Inter-Links/cgi-bin/lists**).

GETTING ACQUAINTED WITH YOUR WEB BROWSER

Your web browser is the client software that is responsible for requesting HTML pages from web servers and then displaying the results. What makes using a web browser so interesting and fun is that by learning a few simple ways of interacting with the program, you can access a world of information and entertainment. The three foundation skills to master with a web browser are entering URLs in the address field, scrolling pages that extend beyond a single screen window, and clicking on hypertext links to navigate. In about 20 seconds, you can practice all three of these skills and know enough to be dangerous. By the end of this section, you will know more about using your web browser skillfully—on purpose!

You actually have three ways to access a web page. First, you can enter a URL from the location field. When you first launch your web browser, it will attempt to connect to the default home page. (In doing so, it may attempt to connect to the Internet if you do not have a live connection and your computer is configured to make a PPP connection.) You can click in the Location field in Navigator (or Address field in Explorer), type the URL, and press the Return key. The web browser will attempt to connect to the site you have entered. If a web address is already present in the location field, you can simply delete the text that appears and enter your own— even while another page is loading.

Set the default home page to a blank page unless you really like to see the same site's page every time you open a new window. Some home pages load quickly, some are graphics-heavy and load quite slowly. If you are in a hurry, you can always cancel a currently loading page by clicking the Stop button in the toolbar or by using a command key equivalent. However, a blank page is the fastest, cleanest way to start. You can set your web browser to open to a blank page in the default dialog box of either browser. When you want to access a web site quickly, use bookmarks.

Second, you can access a bookmarked location. In the same way that a slip of paper in a book helps you return to a chosen page, a web bookmark helps you quickly, conveniently, and accurately return to a web page. It's quick and convenient because all you have to do is pull down a menu and select the name of a web page. Accuracy is important because URLs can be long strings of characters that are not easily remembered, let alone typed!

To create a bookmark, pull down the Bookmarks menu, select Add Bookmark, and the title of the web page currently displayed will be added to the bottom of the list of bookmarks. (Note: this command will not be available if you are on a blank web browser page.) Sometimes the web page authors give titles to their pages that are less descriptive or more verbose than you would like. That's all right, because you can edit the names of your bookmarks and the order in which they are displayed, and you can even create nested displays of your bookmarks around whatever categories you choose.

 Edit your web bookmarks. In Netscape Navigator, you can tidy up your bookmarks. Pull down the Win-

dow menu and select Bookmarks. Each web page that you have bookmarked will appear in a scrolling window.

- *To reorder a bookmark: Drag the bookmark icon up or down the list and drop it in a new position.*
- *To rename a bookmark: Select the bookmark, then pull down the Item menu and choose the Edit Bookmark command. A new window will appear which will allow you to modify the bookmark name, modify its URL, or add to a description of the bookmark. This Edit Bookmark window also displays when the bookmarked site was last visited and when it was created—information that can help you decide whether to keep or delete a bookmark.*
- *To delete a bookmark: Select the bookmark. From the Edit menu, select the Delete Bookmark command. Be careful that you have the right bookmark(s) selected because this command does ask you to verify your selection before taking action. (You can shift-click for multiple selections of bookmarks.) Aside from staying alert, having your bookmarks well organized is the best prevention against inadvertent deletions.*
- *To Organize Bookmarks: Notice the menu choices under the Item menu when your bookmarks are displayed. Use the Insert Separator to create a line between groups of bookmarks. You might have one set of bookmarks for news sites, another for tech support sites, and a third for recreational sites. Use the Insert Folder item to group bookmarks into a hierarchical folder that expands in the browser automatically when it is selected in the Bookmarks menu. If one of your recreational categories was basketball, you might put several sites highlighting your favorite teams in a single folder.*
- *Be sure to close the Bookmark editing window when you are finished organizing, since you will not be able to use Netscape for web browsing until you leave the Bookmark editing window.*

TECH TIP *Here's how to convert between Navigator bookmarks and Explorer favorite places. If you use both Navigator and Explorer, you might find yourself thinking you book-*

marked a site in one browser when you actually marked it in another. The formats the two programs use for storing their web markers are incompatible. So, whether you are synchronizing your bookmarks and favorites or merging them or converting from one browser to another, you should know about utility programs that convert from one format to the other. NavEx is a highly regarded utility for doing this task. You can download NavEx, which is postcardware, from a link found on **techedge.BillRingle.com/resources/***.*

The third way of accessing another web site from a web browser is by clicking on a hypertext link. Remember that a link is represented in text that is underlined and typically in a different color from the other text. Not all underlined text is a hyperlink—it might be the desired text style. Similarly, the web page author might have used colored text to group similar ideas on a page or to have words stand out from the rest of the text. To test whether a piece of text is a hyperlink, place your cursor over the section of text in question and notice whether a web address appears in the status bar, located in the lower left corner of the web browser window. Graphics can also be hyperlinked. Use the same test to determine whether clicking on a graphic will transport your web browser to another location.

TECH TIP *Web browsers have preset colors used to help you differentiate hypertext links that are new from ones that you have visited before. The "classic colors" for hypertext links are blue for a link that has not yet been visited and red for a link that has been explored. You can have any colors you like. You can choose to let the web page override your color preferences or to stick with the colors you have selected. Pull down the Options menu and select the General Preferences command.*

*The window allows you to specify whatever colors you like for
your default link colors.*

Plug-Ins

A plug-in is a file that enhances the capabilities of an application such as a web browser or a graphics program. The plug-
in contains programming code that is usable when the application is launched. Generally, plug-ins are stored in the same
file folder on the hard drive as the application that uses
them. In the Netscape folder, the Default Plug-In file is present to provide a checkpoint for Netscape when it launches.
Any other Netscape plug-ins that are located inside this folder
will also be loaded when Netscape is launched. Plug-ins can
add capabilities to play movies in line with the rest of the
page (rather than pop up a new window just for the movie)
and to play audio recordings as a stream of sound (rather
than download the sound file and use a separate helper application to play the recording) as well as other document and
multimedia capabilities. Best of all, plug-ins can be used by
Explorer as well.

Internet Explorer supports Netscape plug-ins in a similar
fashion. It too has a Plug-In folder at the same directory level
as the Explorer application. When you first install Explorer, it
checks to see if you have a Plug-Ins folder in a Netscape
folder. If so, the Explorer application offers to use the preferences and plug-ins from Netscape.

Three important plug-ins that everyone should have are:

■   QuickTime (**www.quicktime.apple.com**), which dis-
    plays synchronized video and audio. QuickTime VR
    allows the display and manipulation of 3D scenes and
    objects. This can be useful if you wish to offer a short
    action clip of you from the platform.

- Real Audio (**www.realaudio.com**), which allows speech or monaural music to be transmitted over the Internet. Presenters today are using this technology to share short clips of audiotape programs over the Internet for publicity, positioning, and presales reasons.

- Adobe Acrobat (**www.adobe.com**), which provides distribution of documentation in cases where formatting of original documents needs to be preserved. Published newsletters such as TimesFax (an excerpt of the New York Times) as well as the IRS (which distributes its tax forms online) use Acrobat to create documents that can be read online or printed from the web. Acrobat converts documents into a special electronic file called a portable document format, or pdf, file. The greatest advantages of pdf files are that (1) the recipient of a pdf file doesn't need the original application that created the document to read it; (2) any fonts used in the original document are encoded into the pdf file; and (3) pdf files are cross-platform in the widest sense of the term. Pdf viewers for Windows, Macintosh, and Unix platforms can be downloaded from the Adobe web site. Speakers, trainers, and consultants should have ready access to pdf files that they come across on the Internet. You can also consider ways of sharing samples of your published articles and books to enhance your credibility and expertise.

Your best source for learning more about plug-ins and links for downloading them can be found at **www.browser watch.com**. Visit the Plug-In Plaza, where you can view available plug-ins based on the function they perform (video, sound, documentation, or other multimedia) or by platform (Windows 95/97, Windows 3.1, Macintosh, or Unix).

| TECH TIP | *Plug-ins are simple web browser enhancements. You move the ones you want active into the Plug-Ins* |

folder of your web browser prior to launching the browser.

When you encounter special information in a web page that the plug-in is designed to handle, it automatically provides assistance. Plug-ins are not configurable by end users, so what could go wrong? If you run into problems, here are two items to check:

1. *Be sure you are using enough RAM. Plug-ins add to the memory requirements of your web browser. For each plug-in you add, be sure to read the accompanying documentation that advises you on the additional RAM to provide. Mac users can try adding 300 KB to the application memory of your web browser and see whether you get better results loading the particular content supported by the plug-in. See your computer's user's manual for instructions on changing the application RAM.*

2. *Be sure you have the latest version of the plug-in. If you have ample RAM and the content still won't load properly, go to BrowserWatch and see whether you are using the most up-to-date version of the plug-in. It's a simple, but widely overlooked source of a solution.*

SUMMARY

The question What can you do on the Internet? is rapidly turning into the question, What can't you do on the Internet? In Chapter 8, you've assembled your toolkit for getting connected and starting to explore all the possibilities:

■ Dialing into your ISP—how it differs from logging onto an online service

■ E-mail basics: choosing the right e-mail software for you and important features to look for

■ Using nicknames in e-mail to speed your message composition

■ Actions to take with your e-mail—replying, forwarding, sorting, and even deleting when warranted

- Making your e-mail software work for you, using automated filters and responses

- Using pointers to web sites in the mail you receive, and how to make it easy for your recipient to use the pointers you include

- Use e-mail as your personal courier service with attached files

- Customizing the appearance of your e-mail messages using signatures

- Directories, mailing list servers, web browsers, compression software, and more!

Now that you're familiar with the basic tools to use with your ISP account, it's time to make this knowledge work for you in your speaking, training, or consulting pursuits. Chapter 9 will teach you how you can develop high-tech presentations.

 Dig out your business cards and find the ones with e-mail addresses listed. Enter nicknames for those people—friends, clients, suppliers, family, and others to whom you are likely to send e-mail in the next month.

Knowing that people are doing this with business cards, check yours. Is it in need of your e-mail address and web address?

Visit the home page of your browser developer and download the latest version.

Netscape's Navigator or Communicator (**home.netscape.com**)

Microsoft's Internet Explorer (**www.microsoft.com/ie/**)

Presentation Development Using a Computer

Facts, statistics, case studies, surveys, and quotations are just raw material until you arrange them to bring meaning and context for the chosen audience. Technology can help you accomplish this task.

Experienced speakers, trainers, and consultants follow four stages in developing presentations.

1. Topic development
2. Develop the format of the presentation
3. Apply a template and add graphics for visual richness
4. Enhance with multimedia

Let's take a look at each of these stages in greater detail.

STAGE 1: TOPIC DEVELOPMENT

Topic development consists of building your presentation around key points and adding the stories, statistics, exercises, and other material to enrich and support those points.

Organizing the Material into a Presentation

After you have gathered all the background information you need about the topic you are to present, you are ready to tell a story in the form of a presentation.

While every story has a beginning, middle, and end, every presentation has a few overriding objectives. Sample objectives might be to

- explain a new idea
- motivate the audience to take a new course of action
- announce a new product or service
- inform the audience about new facts or industry trends
- remind the audience of important corporate missions or human values
- direct the audience to reflect on progress made in a particular area

One suggested structure for a presentation is:

Introduction
- Presenter
- Objectives

Overview
- Point 1
  supporting evidence
- Point 2
  supporting evidence
- Point 3
  supporting evidence

Call to action and conclusion

Here are two examples of how this top-level outline would look after a first draft. A motivational speech outline might look like the following:

Introduction
- Presenter: Joe Gettum
- Objectives: Seize the opportunities now!

Overview
- My background as a real estate salesman
- Lessons learned in a 20-year career
- If a guy like me who started with nothing can do it, so can you!

Lesson 1: Listen to the customer
- Quote statistics and show graph of listening versus effectiveness
- Jackson Estate story in '77

Lesson 2: Offer to meet their need
- Use rapport skills to speak their language
- Present alternatives
- Give them a choice (story of how I won Commercial Realtor of the Year)

Lesson 3: Follow through and show appreciation
- 5 steps every salesperson should take

Call to action and conclusion
- Listen, think, ask, thank
- Start today and you'll be richer for it!

A product introduction outline might look like the following:

Introduction
- Presenter: Pat Promoter
- Objectives: "Bookmark Magic" boosts your productivity!

Overview
- Relate problem of too many web bookmarks to manage
- Show lack of a strong solution in the marketplace
- Highlight features and benefits of product

Benefit 1: Easy to use
- Nothing is more attractive to users than drag-and-drop
- Demo 4 key areas of "Bookmark Magic"

Benefit 2: Auto analyzer is a smart assistant
- ■ Wouldn't it be great if it knew how you worked?
- ■ Recognizes and sorts based on an expert engine

Benefit 3: Cross-platform for worldwide distribution
- ■ Works on Windows 95, NT, Macintosh, and Solaris
- ■ Simultaneous release in six languages

Call to action and conclusion
- ■ Introductory price
- ■ Demo copies can be downloaded from the Internet
- ■ Go show and tell your customers!

STAGE 2: DEVELOP THE FORMAT OF THE PRESENTATION

This stage of presentation development involves selecting your tools and creating the outline in a presentation software application. Some presenters like to work with a yellow legal sheet or note cards for the outline stage, then type their notes into their computer. Other people are comfortable using computer outline capabilities and prefer to begin with the computer right away. Develop a process built around your work style. There are no right or wrong ways so long as you (and your audiences!) are happy with the results.

While you will find a wealth of tips and tricks in the user manual of your software package, the following overview of each stage will provide a quick-start guide for creating presentation slides.

Tools You Can Use

Following are the most appropriate tools for a presenter to acquire and learn to use because of their powerful features and popularity.

- **Microsoft PowerPoint.** A great package for novice through advanced presenters. Available separately or bundled with Microsoft Office. Best feature is the ability to export a slide show directly as HTML and GIFs to a web site.

- **Adobe Persuasion.** Another powerful package which includes an outliner, slide show, slide sorter, and handout layouts. Graphic tools are more advanced than Power-Point and can export directly to Portable Document Format (PDF) files, which can be shared electronically as files, as printed material, or via the web.

- **Astound's Astound!** A third great presentation package with all the basic features needed for creating and editing slide presentations. What sets Astound apart from the others is advanced multimedia and animation capabilities that do not require programming. In general, Astound does a better job of exporting a slide show to html than Powerpoint.

Creating and Using a Presentation Outline

In any of these presentation software packages, you will be entering text a line at a time for each slide or bullet point. You can use these keyboard short-cuts, toolbar icons, or the pull-down menus to accomplish the same functions.

- Basic editing. Be able to cut, copy, and paste using the Alt (PC) or Command (Macintosh) keys. The Alt and Command keys are generically known as modifier keys, and you use them as you would a shift key to capitalize a letter. Using the appropriate modifier for your computer and the c key copies highlighted text in the presentation software; the modifier and the x key cut highlighted text; and the modifier and the v key paste text to the location designated by the blinking insertion point. This works the same way as any standard word processor.

- New slide. In the outline mode of your presentation package, you press the Return key when you want to create a new line. Each new line you create is typically at the same level as the current line. If you are at the highest level of the outline and you create a new line, you are creating a new slide. The first line of words on a slide is called the slide heading.

■ Changing levels. A slide presentation with only top-level slide headings would be boring. The next part you want to add is the supporting material and bullet points below. After typing the heading and pressing the Return key, press the Tab key to indent the next line. This line of text will appear below the heading and in a smaller-size font than the heading. It may even be a different font from the heading, depending on the template you apply later on. If you want to indent a line further, you can use the Tab key once more; if you want to back up a level, you can use the Delete key to backspace out from the indent.

 At times, you will want to force text to a new line without creating a new bullet point. Hold the Shift key down when you press the Return key to do this. This technique gives you added control over the look of your slides.

TECH TIP *After typing in your outline, save the presentation before going on to the next step!*

Guidelines for Slide Development

To transform an outline into a slide presentation successfully, keep these two guidelines in mind.

1. Balance "Tersity" and Diversity

A slide is not a narrative. It is not meant to be a script, read word for word. Aim for fewer than six lines of text with six words per line. This rule of thumb allows your slide to contain the main heading and several bullet points below without bloating into information overload. If you have that much information to say on a particular point, break the information up into two or more slides. It is even acceptable to put "1 of 5," "2 of 5," and so on in the headline of this particular section of your slides. You'll see this kind of attention to fine detail more commonly in technical training presentations than in other types.

At the most basic level, each slide is meant to frame your speaking points. For instance, when you see the phrase "Be a TEAM" on the screen, your memory is jogged and you explain that the acronym stands for "Together Everyone Achieves More" and share some relevant examples. Remember, phrases work better than sentences, except in the case of accurate quotations.

Variety is important in your slides—whether you have 5 or 50 slides in your presentation. The first and last slides should be used to introduce and reinforce your theme, usually by presenting the title of your talk. The first slide provokes curiosity and stimulates relevancy; when seen as the final slide, the title can recall the advice and recommendations made in the presentation.

2. Make the Text Readable

The words in your outline must be large enough to be read easily in the back of the room. Remember the six-by-six rule you may have learned in the audio-visual unit of a public speaking course—no more than six words horizontally; no more than six items on the page. The graphics, likewise, should convey their meaning readily. If a graphic is too small, it may appear to the people farthest away simply as a blob.

STAGE 3: APPLY A TEMPLATE AND ADD GRAPHICS FOR VISUAL RICHNESS

Once you have your outline shown as slides, you'll notice that they look quite plain. In order to spruce up the look and feel of your document, you will want to apply a template.

From within your presentation package, select an auto template. This action will present you with a list of professionally designed formats for presenting your information. You will be able to select from several dozen master elements and color schemes for "video screen," or "overheads," or "35 mm slides." Each of the categories contains the same templates using different aspect fonts and colors with the different target mediums (screen display, transparency slide, or paper) in mind.

Since you can reapply a template at any time, start by selecting from the color overheads family of templates as you design your presentation. Then, when you want to use it to create handouts, you can select black-and-white overheads with the same style template and print them out. If you need 35 mm slides produced, select the corresponding template from that family. For slide output, you can send your finished presentation file to a slide bureau, a service company that specializes in producing 35mm slides (if there are no slide bureaus in your area, you can use a mail-order firm such as Genigraphics). Slide bureaus take the electronic file and turn each slide into a mounted 35 mm slide for use with a projector.

Use Color Contrasts to Your Advantage

Light blue letters on a dark blue background, no matter how sublime it appears at your desktop, become nearly invisible when projected on screen. Stick to proven color schemes. Microsoft PowerPoint and Adobe Persuasion make recommendations for sharp contrasts between text and background in their style templates. Unless you have a compelling reason, follow these simple guidelines: (1) The brightest part of the slide will be the most eye-catching in a dark room. For this reason, white or yellow text on a dark shade of blue or red background is widely used. (2) Avoid distracting graphical backgrounds. Gradients, overwhelming colors, and gratuitous graphics can all diminish attention placed on your message. Use graphics to enhance your message, illustrate an idea, or emphasize a point.

Lines that are too thin or text that is too small on a diagram can also hurt your presentation. You can spot this during your run-through and tech check on stage. Be sure to have the software needed to edit if necessary. It is short-sighted to bring only the player software to the event; install the full version of the presentation package on your hard drive so you can make changes as necessary.

Guidelines for Slide Templates

On a slide-by-slide basis, use a consistent style and background. This allows the participants to develop a readiness to expect information in a certain format and establishes the presentation look and feel.

Fonts are the particular typefaces used in a document. You are probably familiar with many of the font names from your experience with word processing. Sans serif fonts (in other words, fonts without curlicues) are better used for headings than for lower-level text. These fonts have straighter lines on each character and show up well in bold and large font sizes. Arial or Helvetica are examples of sans serif fonts.

Other fonts have more definition and work better visually where the words are more plentiful and the reader's eye has more "texture" to grasp. These fonts are called serif fonts, of which Times and Courier are examples.

Exercise
Look at a newspaper or well-designed newsletter and examine the differences between the headline fonts and the fonts used in the articles. Can you pick out the sans serif and serif fonts?

Adding Visual Variety

You can add interesting elements to vary the appearance of significant slides. For example, when comparing an old way of answering the telephone with a new way, you can make a side-by-side chart and highlight the benefits of your proposed change. You can use diagrams, flowcharts, and graphs to illustrate your ideas and make them more memorable to your audience. Persuasion, PowerPoint, and Astound! all come with terrific clip art packages which allow you to select, modify, and place professional-quality graphics into your slides.

If you have access to a scanner, you can add cartoons, magazine and newspaper headlines, and photographs. Consider the added impact you have when you say, "Society struggles daily with conflict," and the slide that you present has big, bold headlines and magazine cover stories that reference jury trials, law suits, strikes, and consumer safety complaints.

Naturally, you cite sources for your materials. To avoid complications over copyright issues, I recommend that when you use something like a cartoon strip in your overhead, you always check with the copyright holder and get written permission before using the material.

Use Blank Space and Blank Slides Purposefully

Remember that your slides are not the focus of your presentation. You are the most important delivery mechanism for your message. When you want to shift the audience's attention from the screen to yourself, intersperse a slide without words or pictures. Doing this is the high-tech equivalent of putting a cardboard cover on an overhead projector.

An added benefit for the participants of doing this is that they get to move their necks to a new, lower, and more relaxed position. If your audience is less tense, it is also more receptive to your message because it has more attention available to consider your message.

Employ Progressive Disclosure

Progressive disclosure is simply showing relevant portions of material on a slide as appropriate. It is sometimes called the reveal technique. As a high school math teacher, I used to use a form of progressive disclosure all the time by explaining calculus solutions and geometric proofs one line at a time by sliding a piece of paper down as I described each step to the class. When I became a professional trainer, I learned the terminology and realized the value of the technique for focusing attention with adult audiences as well.

You should be familiar with two basic forms of progressive disclosure. The first is when you have a long list of bullet items to cover under a topic point or simply want to control how much the audience sees of the points at one time (for building anticipation or preventing a punch line from being given away). Second, you should be able to use this technique with graphics with the layering command. This is a great technique for showing before-and-after slides or pros and cons.

Technology facilitates your use of progressive disclosure. It is cleaner, more accurate, and more professional than doing it manually. When you are speaking to a very large audience with a ceiling-mounted or back-lit projection system, this is the only way to go. However, if you are in a bind and using an overhead, you can always fall back to using a sheet of paper to cover up portions you don't want the audience to see until the right moment for maximum impact.

Also, do not confuse progressive disclosure with slide transitions, which are visual effects that add a sense of movement between electronic slides. The movement could be a wipe to the left while the next slide in a series appears to slide in from the right side of the screen and cover the previous slide. Slide transitions in combination with progressive disclosure can work well; used alone, transition effects may be overused, may be cumbersome, and may add little value to a presentation. Be sure to rehearse if you use slide transitions to make sure the timing does not throw your rhythm off.

TECH TIP **Build in Nonlinear Jump Points**

Without getting too fancy, you can add significant depth to a presentation by using jump points. A jump point is a mechanism that allows you to skip around in the order of your presentation, making the slides more like index cards which can be reshuffled than like bound pages in a book. Often, the ability to shift one or more slides around is very desirable when reworking a presentation to strengthen or streamline it. Adding jump points allows you to save content in the presentation file and use it on an as needed basis.

For example, in my presentation of "Driver's Ed for the Information Superhighway," I make the assumption that most business audiences have heard all they care to on the history, costs, and policies of the Internet, so I just have one slide with a few bullet points for each of those topics. However, if I encounter an audience that wants or needs to know details of the evolution of internetworking, I click on a jump point on the history slide and have a time line that shows the four research institutions that were the first Internet hosts and what services they offered in 1969. Then, we can trace the history from that point forward to the present through several slides, with the ability to jump back to the main presentation at any point.

Creating jump points is relatively easy in Persuasion, PowerPoint, and Astound! You simply designate a graphic as your jump point button on a particular slide and then select the destination slide, or where you want to land when you jump from the original slide. You can have more than one jump point per slide. This is handy if you have three important topics on a slide and you want to have the ability to go into more depth on any of them individually based upon comments or questions that members of the audience raise.

STAGE 4: ENHANCE WITH MULTIMEDIA

If you learn one thing about using multimedia (sound, graphics, animation) in a presentation, let it be this: there is a huge difference between just enough and too much!

It is understandable and commendable to want to liven up your message with pictures and music, but the very fine line between "adding enough to spice up the presentation" and "overpowering" is often trampled by enthusiastic presenters.

Use Multimedia, Not MULTIMEDIA

I've seen some of the best and worst in the business. Multimedia presentations at their best incorporate appropriate, relevant graphics, sound, and animation to support, elaborate, and focus the point of the speaker's message.

■   When talking about the difference a new product will make, you might show a cost-analysis graph indicating the scenarios and the benefits to customers.

- When making a point about a computer dialog box that needs to be responded to in a particular way, show the dialog box in your slides with the correct settings.

- When boasting about a result of a new staff program, resist the urge to tell the story yourself. Instead, videotape members of the staff telling the story in their own words for even greater credibility. You can project the video separately or digitize it and incorporate the clip into your slides.

- When describing how close communications helped staff avoid dangers, you might illustrate the point with a short movie clip of your group successfully rafting white-water rapids to highlight the importance of reacting quickly to changing conditions and of everyone going in the same direction.

- When underscoring the importance of showing appreciation for family and friends, you might use a picture backdrop on a single slide of birthday parties, graduations, weddings, or even funerals, depending on the emotional tone that supports your message.

In general, avoid letting the multimedia speak for you. Instead, the slides should act as a stage setting for your presentation. You know you have crossed the line if you

- neglect to rehearse with the slides, because then your timing will be off;

- notice that the audience is laughing in the wrong places because they find your gimmick transitions and sound effects more entertaining and interesting than your message;

- find yourself getting caught up in the presentation display as an observer rather than as a presenter; or

- get asked why you used a graphic on *every* slide.

Fortunately, examples of multimedia gross excess and irrelevance are uncommon. Usually, the opposite problem is more common: speakers, trainers, and consultants lack the necessary graphics background and experience and are reluctant to dabble in an area that they know little about. Depending on your audience, experience, and the kind of time and money you want to invest, you have two choices. Either you can develop these skills yourself or you can hire a professional graphics artist to work with you to create the desired effects. Often, spending $20 to $30 per hour for a few days' time with an experienced graphics artist/illustrator will produce outstanding results that will pay off the next time you present with those materials.

Create Slide Workbooks for Participants

Your presentation software also has the ability to produce workbooks from the slides. It accomplishes this task by reducing the size of the slide and leaving room on the page for you to customize it with your header, footer, and notes for the participants. Workbooks produced from this software can range from very simple to very complex, depending on the time and effort you devote to the project.

The two most significant benefits of creating participant workbooks are that (1) you reinforce the learning of the participants because they have another medium to interact with. In addition to listening to you and seeing the slides, they have a workbook in which to write their own insights and applications of your presentation. After the presentation, additional recall of the material is aided by the workbook. (2) Participants have more attention available for your presentation when they have a well-designed notebook with valuable content. If they have the information from the slides, they will not need to write down as many notes from your talk. Thus, they can realize one of the most critical benefits of a presentation, which is enjoying the experience and having the opportunity to reflect on the message.

TECH TIP *Your audience might benefit from your creating a separate version of your slide workbook that is a carefully selected subset of your larger presentation:*

1. *In a sales presentation, you want to leave behind a focused handout of your major points. The workbook will help participants evaluate choices; it will not complete the sale on its own. Respect the intelligence of your customers as well as their time.*
2. *You might create a different set of notes for your presenters that includes checklists, suggested exercises to increase audience involvement, and additional background material to help whoever is presenting answer more in-depth questions.*

SUMMARY

The online world can bring you tons of research information, but to turn it into a coherent and interesting presentation, you need to disconnect and focus on your topic. Chapter 9 has shown you

- which software to use when making slides for your presentation;
- how to format the individual slides in your presentation, and how best to provide transitions among them; and
- good practices to follow (and pitfalls to avoid!) when adding multimedia "sizzle" to your presentation.

You've turned your online research into presentation topics, developed into slides. Now, how do you prepare for and deliver the presentation? Chapter 10 will teach you how to present with technology.

Review the current versions of PowerPoint, Persuasion, and Astound! Are you currently using the software that will best serve your needs? Do you anticipate those needs changing in the next 12 months as more of your competition explores ways to embellish presentations using high-tech techniques?

Using a set of slides that you have created, look for opportunities to create nonlinear jump points to more depth. Practice using them so that when you need to use one in front of a group, you will be confident enough to do so.

10 Preparing, Presenting, and Follow-Up

This chapter will help you plan and deliver high-tech presentations by familiarizing you with the issues involved and making recommendations on ways to avoid problems on the platform. Confidence with your tools will help you deliver more persuasive presentations. The observation that Murphy was an optimist was certainly made by a high-tech presenter. You will learn that the most critical element of using technology to present is thorough preparation.

PREPARING

The five most important aspects of planning a high-tech presentation are as follows:

Be Familiar with Your Equipment

You can present with technology that you own, that someone else owns, or that is a combination of the two. At sites that you have visited before, you might feel comfortable bringing just the presentation file. Teaching a university course in the same room week after week is an example of when you can rely on the equipment being of a certain caliber: you know the computer, the projection system, the screen, the lighting, and the installed software. All you would need to bring (or to be able to access via a campus network from your office) is the presentation file and fonts.

You will encounter a variety of microphones in your speaking career, from a gooseneck podium microphone to a omnidirectional boom mike used on movie sets. For the full-time or part-time speaker, it's a good idea to own a simple microphone and amplifier system in case the meeting planner cannot provide one. Use the overview of microphones in Chapter 1 as a basis for communicating your needs to the technical crew or other support staff.

The next three tips deal with using computer slides in a presentation.

Master Your Software—Sufficiently Well

Let's make an important distinction regarding proficiency. You don't have to know your presentation software down to every last feature. You do have to know about the features you are going to use. Avoid paralysis from over-analysis, but do be competent in the skill areas on which you will be depending in your presentations.

Many times, computer users will get turned off by reading the technical reference manual for a product because it is poorly written or above their heads. Do not let that stop you from learning! When you have bookstores, telephone support, user groups, and tech support online, you have no excuse for not using your software and using it well.

Create an Alias or Shortcut to the Desktop Window

A point will come after your introduction when you wish to start your presentation using the computer. At that time, you want the transition to be quick, smooth, and trouble-free. The worst thing you can do in front of an audience is to click through layers of folders searching for a file. Episodes like this create an impression in the audience's mind that the presenter is poorly organized and lead to anxiety for the presenter.

One solution to this problem is to have your presentation slides open and running on the computer. For various reasons, however, you might not have the time to preload the slides. Then you will need a quick way to access your file without having to hunt for it on your hard drive. Moving the presentation file to your desktop is another solution, but that can disrupt links from the presentation to other files (such as movies, audio clips, and so on). The Windows operating system is especially fragile when it comes to moving files from one subdirectory to another. A better way to make the file accessible from the desktop is to create a shortcut, or alias, to the file.

A shortcut is like a note on the kitchen table that tells you that your sandwich is in the refrigerator. The note is not the sandwich, it simply tells you where to go to get the sandwich. In the meantime, the sandwich can stay fresh and not spoil by staying in the refrigerator.

Here's how to create this type of "pointer-to-a-file" file on the three major platforms:

Using Windows 3.1, you can create a shortcut by following these steps:
1. Select the File menu
2. Find the file in the File Manager
3. In the dialog box, fill in the name for the shortcut and a group name
4. Save the shortcut appropriately

Using Windows 95:
1. Right-click on the presentation file
2. Select the choice to make a shortcut
3. Save the file to the desktop
4. Position the file so that it is not covered by windows and is easily accessible

Using the Macintosh:

1. Select the presentation file
2. Select the Alias command from the File menu; an alias appears next to the file
3. Drag the alias to the desired position on the desktop

Exit and Reenter the Presentation Gracefully

One way to shift the focus of your audience is to put in "blank" slides. This works well for 35 mm or computer slides. With computer slide presentations, you want to be able to switch to another application during your presentation. You might want to launch a spreadsheet or a web browser to illustrate a point or demonstrate a technique. Be sure you can get out of your slide presentation, into the new application, and back to the right spot in your slide presentation.

The best advice for switching between applications is to have all the applications you are going to use running before you start your presentation. (As a backup plan, have shortcuts or aliases to the documents and/or applications on your desktop.)

In Windows, you can use the Alt–Tab key combination to switch between active applications. On the Macintosh, you can switch between applications by using the applications icon in the upper right corner of the menu bar. The keyboard combination is faster when you only have one or two programs you are switching between; the menu bar selection is better in that you will not have to cycle through several programs to get to the one you need.

TECH TIP *In PowerPoint, you can fade your presentation to black or white as a transition effect when switching to another program. (Here's one instance where the delay caused by a transition effect is desirable.) Press Alt–b to fade your presentation to a black screen and Alt–w. (Mac users sub-*

stitute the Command key for the Alt key.) Repeating the command–key sequence will undo the effect.

Contact the A/V Site Crew in Advance

The site crew is the person or persons who will be at the presentation location to help you with your equipment needs. A site crew member might go by the title Audio-Video Specialist, Systems Engineer, or, "I'm Fred. People call me when they have technical problems in the auditorium."

You want to contact the A/V site crew as soon as you book an engagement. Tell the person in charge the date, time, length of your presentation, and your technical equipment needs. Ask and answer questions to get a complete picture of what will be possible with the equipment at the location, as well as what will be possible if you bring/rent equipment yourself. Some presenters put standard clauses into their contracts requiring the client to provide access to necessary equipment and services. You have to decide for yourself what is required and what is negotiable.

For example, if you are asked to deliver to a group of a hundred people in an after-dinner address, you know you will need a microphone to be heard above the dessert spoons and coffee cups. You need to decide what you are comfortable with and make sure that the client or sponsor can provide that. Some professionals feel perfectly comfortable addressing a group from behind a podium or lectern because of the stability and sense of security it provides. A lectern microphone offers simple, reliable control over amplification. It generally picks up your voice very well with fast, minor adjustments to the gooseneck that positions the distance of the microphone from the speaker's mouth.

Others want a hand-held mike with a very long cord that allows them to walk around the floor and interact with the audience. These folks like to be hard-wired to the facility sound system and don't mind using one hand to hold the microphone. With a hand-held mike, you need to become very skilled at holding the microphone consistently close enough to your mouth to have it amplify your voice properly but not so close that the mike interjects hissing or covers your facial expressions.

Another type of speaker favors the freedom that a wireless microphone gives. By simply clipping a transmitter to your pocket or belt, you can now switch your power on or off, and this arrangement frees up your hands for gesturing or operating other props.

Different venues require different technology. Several times I've used headset microphones when presenting on a convention show floor where there was a lot of background noise and having hands free was desirable to demonstrate points on a computer. When this works, it saves your voice tremendously over the course of a day. Problems can arise when the headset starts to slide, either because you moved beyond the range of the lead cord or the headset itself loosens up.

Other issues to discuss with the A/V site crew include:

- Positioning of the stage podium or presenter's table
- The locations of the nearest electrical outlets
- Who is responsible for having spare projector bulbs
- Video or audio recording arrangements
- Network or phone access, and any configuration information

TECH TIP *As a rule of thumb, do not ask any member of the site crew about logistical details such as airport shuttles, the location of the photocopier, or to get you water. These details are the responsibility of the meeting planner, and you* *risk offending the technician. All kidding aside, the technical support staff often gets little credit for saving the day for many presenters.*

Travel Wisely with Equipment

One of the disadvantages of having technology that you are familiar with is that you have to get it to the site where you are presenting. You can either ship it or lug it around with you. Here is a short list of tips for travel cases as well as tools to bring. The essentials are so important to my work that I've found ways to travel with them everywhere.

Tips for Computer Bags

A computer bag is the most important component of your traveling equipment. Be sure to get a bag that has room for folders and files, extra pockets for tools and cables and a spare notebook battery, and still has room to spare. The clamshell cases open on your lap. I prefer the top-loading cases which require you to take the computer out before using it; these types of cases are less prone to spilling papers and other items in bumpy plane and taxi rides.

- Targus bags are good, low-end bags, costing less than $100. I used them for years. About every year, I'd wear through the zipper or the bag would start to look worn out and need replacing.
- Port Technology bags cost less than $200, depending on the model you choose. These are the best bags I've ever owned. The handles are comfortable even with 35 pounds of equipment inside, and the zippers are super-sturdy.

Additional Tools to Bring
- Plug adapters
- Power strip, power cord

- Modem users: long RJ-32 cable for hooking up to the hotel phone
- Network users: spare patch cord with RJ-45 ends for Ethernet wires
- Extension cord—3-foot
- Electrical tape
- Tool kit with small screwdrivers, pliers, wire cutters
- Low-tech gear:
  - Black and red magic markers for paper
  - Water soluble marking pens for overhead transparencies
  - Duct tape for securing wires to the floor

Preparing your Notebook Computer for Travel

Many people wonder whether airport security x rays can damage their computers or disks. It's a good question, and one which I have looked into over the years. Reports say that magnetic media won't be affected due to the wavelength of the x-ray devices. As a precaution, store a copy of your presentation on a disk in addition to the version on the hard drive. You should know that photographic negatives are affected to varying degrees by airport x-ray machines. Some of the effects are not noticeable at the time of development, but some are.

TECH TIP *Mail photographic negatives to your office or destination for safety. Also, you can mail your presentations to yourself via e-mail as a double backup plan.*

Learn to put your computer into sleep mode before leaving for the airport if you plan on using it early on in the flight. Sleep mode is a low-energy consumption state that has a minimal impact on the battery power of the computer. A computer in sleep mode "wakes up" faster at security checkpoints since it does not have to completely load the operating system, only reactivate the screen and display.

Computer batteries come in two basic varieties: nickel-cadmium (NiCd) and lithium-ion (Li). The nickel batteries last between one and a half and two hours under typical use, the lithium batteries last about twice as long. Newer (and more expensive) notebooks use the lithium batteries.

If you are going on a cross-country flight and need to use the computer, be sure to bring along a spare battery. At layover points, take advantage of the wall outlets to recharge your batteries. Lastly, avoid presenting from a battery which may cause the computer to report low energy readings during your talk. Use the battery only as a last resort backup to presenting with an electrical power connection.

Airport Security

Meeting planners are not the only ones who have noticed more speakers, trainers, and consultants traveling with laptop computers these days; unfortunately, airport thieves have as well. Because of their high value and low weight, laptops are a prime target. Here are four common areas where a snatch can occur and several tips on how to avoid a loss.

First, be aware of checking bags outside the terminal, where a well-dressed crook can walk up to unattended luggage and walk away unnoticed. Like most speakers, I tote my PowerBook and overnight bag with me onto the plane and only check luggage when it exceeds the carry-on limit. If you do check a bag at curbside, be sure the attendant puts it on the conveyer belt or behind the counter.

The second place to be cautious is at the ticket counter because there is a good chance that your attention will be diverted from your bags while you are talking to the ticket agent. The prevention tip here is if you need to put your computer down, put it on top of the counter where you can keep an eye on it, or put your foot on the strap if you must put it on the ground.

The third place is at the security checkpoint, where you and your bags must pass through a metal detector. A common ploy for a team of thieves is to wait until you've put your computer bag on the conveyor belt and to cause a delay by setting off the metal detector. You become delayed and distracted by the commotion while your bag is picked up on the other side of the metal detector by an accomplice. Never let anyone cut in front of you once you've put your articles on the belt.

The fourth trouble spot is in the gateway area, where people tend to let their guard down because they are past the security checkpoint. Don't leave any valuables on a seat while you make a quick phone call, check departure times, or grab a pretzel. If you turn your back on your computer bag, it may be the last time you see it.

Remember, it's worth the extra trouble to be safe. It's not just your equipment that's at stake, but your presentation, contact names and numbers, e-mail, and all your other work in progress on the computer.

Arrive in Tme to Connect and Test Equipment

Never assume that you can walk up, plug in, and begin talking if your presentation involves using electricity. An increasingly popular trend in software industry trade shows is to have special presentations for invited audiences. Typically, a day before a big convention, a company will sponsor a room and invite presenters to address their areas of specialty for 45 minutes, take a few questions, and then let the next presenter take the stage. It's a great arrangement for the audience, because they get a variety of different topics, perspectives, and styles to learn from. It's great for the sponsor, because the cost to them is minimal and they usually bring in industry experts who tell success stories using the company's products. It's challenging as a presenter because of the tag-team nature of the presentations and the limited time for set-up and testing.

At one of these events at the Anna Hotel in San Francisco, the presentation machine was hooked up to an LCD projector that sat on an overhead. The plan was for presenters to walk up, load their presentation into the machine from a diskette, Zip drive, or hard drive, double-click, and begin. The sponsoring company had loaded PowerPoint and Persuasion on the hard drive. When the third speaker got up to load his presentation, he found out that he had used a noncompatible version of PowerPoint. The story turned out all right—he was able to boot up from his laptop computer by hooking the video output port directly into the projector system, and after 10 minutes, the presentation was back on track.

In smaller meetings (less than 20 people), you might encounter large screen televisions for your display amplification. VGA-NTSC devices exist which convert the video signal produced from either a PC or Macintosh into a signal format that can be displayed on a television screen.

If you are invited to participate in an event where you use equipment set up by others, remember the value of a little advance communication. Find out the software and versions that will be loaded in advance on the presentation computer. If necessary, create or modify your slides to work with the target configuration. It's the easiest, least stressful solution in the long run.

In a similar vein, be sure to use standard fonts. It will ensure a greater chance of full compatibility. At the end of the day, no one in the audience will be concerned that you didn't use some spiffy, subtle fonts. They will remember the riveting delivery and high-value information you delivered.

Be Familiar with the Presentation Room

Control the Climate

This is a practical measure that should become second nature to every speaker, trainer, and consultant. When you enter a room where you will be working, notice the location of the lighting switches and thermostat. Too often, people assume that others will either take care of a problem if one arises or that the participants won't notice if the temperature is too hot or too cold.

Being a true professional means going beyond the expected. I've seen some real pros take time to discuss their requirements with the food serving staff in advance and ask for their cooperation. I've also watched speakers who wanted to reduce the noise in the room go so far as to tape foam in door jambs to soften the sound of doors closing during the speech.

Master the Lights

Neglecting to learn the lighting system is not a bright idea. If you can get to the presentation room before partici-pants arrive, experiment with the lights so you know exactly how to create the lighting level you require. At the time you need to change the lights, you may not be the closest one to the controls. Knowing in advance which switches need to be in what position allows you to direct an assistant to help you get just the effect you desire.

Sometimes learning your lighting system is as simple as finding out which switch controls which bank of lights and being able to turn off the front set of lights when your pre-sentation requires the use of a screen. Sometimes, stage light-ing is preset into control panel buttons activated from the podium. Commonly, you will find a full light and a full dark setting as well as two or three in between. The best practice is setting your equipment up and finding out which lighting setting best suits your need based upon the most light you can have to allow visual interaction with the participants while still being able to see the material on the screen clearly from the back of the room.

Lastly, it is important to remember how to turn on the lights after a period of dimmed light without jarring your audience. Flipping on the lights abruptly at the end of a training session is not doing your audience a favor. It is better to tell them that you'll be bringing up the lights now for the break and to do so gradually.

Having someone else control your lights can result in having them come on too soon or too suddenly as well. Simplify. Spend five minutes learning the lights.

Setting Up the Seating

During a presentation that lasts an hour or more, you would be wise to provide the best seating arrangements for your participants. The less they have to turn their heads to watch you and see your slides, the more comfortable they will be and the more receptive they will be to your message. Test the seating provided for you by sitting in the outermost seats with your equipment turned on, and feel free to move the chairs or have them moved.

PRESENTING

End on Time

This is a low-tech tip, but one that becomes even more easily overlooked when using high tech to present. Regardless of the circumstances, end on or before the time you have been allotted. Here are a few tips to help you keep on track:

- Set a clock so you can see it comfortably. This can range from taking your wristwatch off and setting it on the podium to buying a travel clock with large digital numbers that can be seen from the floor. Do whatever you must do to keep track of the time, especially if you are one of several speakers presenting from the same platform.

- Time your rehearsals. One way to hone your skills is to practice in a highly structured environment. You can arrange this in your own home or office, but there is nothing to compare to giving a short speech before a live audience. Join Toastmasters to develop your skills in this area, or give a showcase presentation at your local NSA chapter.

- Have summary materials to cover points without going into complete detail. Paying attention to your audience, staying flexible, allowing time for interaction, answering questions and listening to concerns are all ways to provide additional value to your audiences as a presenter. They are also variables that affect the length of time you have to spend on your prepared material. Regardless of whether or how you provide time for these audience interactions, you are ultimately responsible for ending on time. It is a matter of professional discipline and reputation. As such, you should have ways of abbreviating your presentation that are congruent with your level of experience. Again, planning is the key to success in giving an 8-minute explanation or story in 30 seconds.

Quotations are a favorite way of capturing the essence of material when you are in a time crunch. For instance, saying, "Time is God's way of keeping everything from happening at once," can substitute for an interesting but noncritical explanation of a long process. If a participant wants to hear the details, be sure to provide a way for him or her to contact you following the presentation.

Never Let the Slides Become the Focus

Remember that you are the presenter, the deliverer of the message. Your slides are there to assist you, not the other way around!

One presenter during a break-out session of a convention had added random sounds to every one of his slide transitions. As he advanced from his introductory slide to his overview, a "boo" emitted from the loud speakers. When he clicked on the next slide, we all heard a jarring "beep." On his third slide transition, we heard a digitized screech of car tires. To make matters worse, the presenter noticed a few participants giggling at the transition noises and remarked, "I can't help it. I do this for a living." The poor fellow neglected the 95 percent of the room that was cringing in the dark as each slide advanced. Furthermore, he failed to realize that he was sacrificing his credibility for the sake of cuteness.

Equipment Interruptions

In the summer of 1989, I was teaching a word processing course for administrative staff at a university. I was at the point of my training where I was explaining Ringle's third rule of word processing, which is "Save early and save often," when a participant got up to go to the bathroom. Accidentally, as she made her way out, she stumbled on a power cord and disrupted power for a row of eight computers. As an instructor, I couldn't have asked for a better example to motivate students to action!

Equipment can hang you up without any help from people. Have you ever had an extension cord that was two inches too short for where you wanted to move a projector? Have you had a three-prong plug to put into a wall socket that only had two-prong outlets?

When you are being hired, you should ask to speak to whoever is responsible for the room you will be working in. Ask all the questions you can think of about equipment. Also ask about a backup plan: "What if we needed another extension cord? Is that something that would be easy for you to bring along or should I do that?"

Use a Microphone

Whether you feel like using a microphone or not, it helps whenever you address more than 20 people at a time. This is especially true where there is a high likelihood of background noise, such as spoons stirring coffee or doors closing during a dinner presentation.

Have a Backup Strategy in Case of Microphone Failure

Once you decide to use a microphone, be sure to create a backup plan. Doing so will distinguish you as a real pro. During the 1995 NSA Convention in Minneapolis, I saw Mike McKinley addressing a crowd of nearly two thousand professional speakers. This is an unusual circumstance, one filled with the potential for making a memorable impression for better or worse. He was wearing a wireless microphone when the battery pack failed midsentence. Mike walked over to the side of the stage and was handed a wired microphone. He continued to speak while a technician came from back stage and replaced the battery pack that was attached to his belt. In less than a minute, Mike got a nod from the technician that the replacement microphone was operational, so he handed back the wired microphone and continued speaking without missing a beat.

Well-executed maneuvers like this do not occur without prior planning. At NSA Conventions, you can pick up a great many tips like this that clearly demonstrate what it means to be a professional speaker!

Overcome the Unexpected

No matter how thoroughly you plan and prepare, you always have to leave room for the unexpected to occur. Don't think of it as bad luck when the fire alarm erupts in the middle of your talk. The best way to deal with it is with grace and a sense of humor.

Tony Robbins presented "Successful Selling Strategies" at the Valley Forge Convention Center in Pennsylvania in 1993. When he was in the middle of acting out a story on stage in front of more than two thousand businesspeople, his right shoe flew off his foot and over his head. Tony dealt with the situation like the pro he is—at first, a look of surprise crossed his face, then he just smiled a big grin, incorporated a missing shoe into his story, and completed it. One of the stage crew retrieved the shoe and Tony was able to slip it on the next time he walked back to put another slide on his overhead projector.

Part of the fun and excitement with presenting is that it happens in real time. There are real risks. A good presentation is never a monologue, but a dialogue with audience members. Without their reactions, their laughter, their contributions, it wouldn't be the same. Live presentations are meant to be different—otherwise we'd all just record audio and video tapes.

Prepare to Deal with Difficult Equipment

What kinds of things go wrong with a presentation involving high technology? Everything you can imagine. Projection bulbs blow out. Screens fall. Staging drops. Microphones squeak. Hard drives crash. Software conflicts or fails to load. Fonts disappear. Adapter cables fail to adapt. And any web site you want to show live during a presentation can be busier than usual, down for repairs, or have suddenly implemented a new log-in procedure. It's all part of the challenge and the fun.

So, how do you approach presenting with technology that can be so sensitive and capricious? Start with an attitude of expectation.

1. Expect that something will go wrong.
2. Expect that you can handle whatever goes wrong.

Then, have some one-liners to stay in control of the situation. Professional seminar leader on humor and convention presenter Tom Antion provides a wealth of information on how to "bomb proof" your presentations with the use of humor in his book, *Wake 'Em Up Business Presentations*. For instance, if a participant calls attention to a spelling error in your slides, Tom offers five ways to respond:

- As Mark Twain once said, "I don't give a damn for a man who can't spell a word only one way."
- Oh! I apologize. My word processor has a virus.
- That is the Swahili/pig Latin spelling.
- That was put there to test you.
- I knew I shouldn't have had my dog proofread this.

Of course, you make the correction following the presentation, but in the meantime, you maintain your poise and focus. The worst mistake you can make is to lose sight of your audience's needs.

In the case of a serious technical difficulty, you may opt to take an early break. If you are conducting a half-day or longer program, you can take a 15-minute "bio break." In any shorter presentation, abandon the problem, fall back to whatever is working, and go on from there. The audience cares about your presentation, which is only aided by the technology.

Have Enough Materials for Distribution

In every presentation you deliver, no matter to what audience or on what topic, you should always distribute a handout to the participants—for three reasons. First, writing your thoughts down for a handout helps focus your presentation and will improve the quality of your delivery. Second, it adds value for the participants to have a physical take-away of your material. It strengthens their learning and is an opportunity to reinforce your message. Lastly, a handout acts as a marketing tool for your business. Be sure to put your contact information on every piece of material that you create.

Now that we've established the necessity of a handout, always create 15 percent more than the number of participants that you expect. If 200 people are registered, request that 230 copies of the workshop materials be prepared. Here is how this will benefit your business:

1. You are prepared for more people showing up. Because you have materials for them, they will feel welcomed, and you will look like a true pro for being prepared.

2. You are able to allow a few participants to take more than one at the end of the presentation. Make your handouts something special in themselves through the use of graphics and multiple colors and participants will appreciate the professional quality. They will also be more likely to save your materials for reference or pass them along to a supervisor or colleague.

3. You should put a purchase price on the back of a multi-page handout. Doing so represents value to both the participant and the creator. It took time and effort to produce, and that should be recognized. If you are an NSA member, discuss strategies with other professional presenters at your chapter for placement and positioning of your materials. Comparing your materials to other people's materials will help you get a feel for what level of quality and depth is expected for a given value range.

4. Extras should be filed back at the office and reused in part or in whole. An excellent way to get lasting value from a handout is to include a variety of them in your marketing materials, proposals, and targeted marketing campaigns.

FOLLOW UP A PRESENTATION

Evaluate Your Presentation

Following each presentation, you have the opportunity to learn from your results and improve. If you neglect to perform an honest, thorough evaluation of how things went, you are neglecting to reap a significant value from the experience.

At a minimum, ask yourself these questions:

- What went right? Acknowledge what worked well from both a delivery perspective and technical viewpoint. Did you implement a new plan or piece of equipment? Which slides, effects, or demonstrations got the best response?
- What needs to be improved? Here is where you look at the things that needed to happen but for some reason did not. Were you unable to get to the site in time to preload and test your software? After each of these points, consider what behavior within your control you can change to make these things happen in the future.
- How can it become even better? This area involves not just the things that went well or the things you know you need to do better but goes beyond to tap into resources and ideas that could be integrated to bring you to the next level. As with most things, it is the small incremental steps that lead you to greater success. What should be added to make the presentation even better?

Show Appreciation for the Opportunity

Use your computer or a notepad to send a thank you note within a week of each presentation to the meeting planner.

Notes such as these are appreciated and remembered. If a technical support person or crew were instrumental in helping your presentation, be sure to include them in your list of people to thank.

SUMMARY

In this chapter, you learned how to make yourself comfortable when presenting as well as how to ensure that your audience will be comfortable when listening to you. Achieving this comfort level takes careful planning.

- Choose the right audio system for the setting (podium, hand-held, or headset microphone)
- Make sure your laptop computer arrives with you, wherever you're going
- Scope out the scene at the presentation room or auditorium—ascertain where to plug in your gear, control the room lighting and temperature, configure the seating
- Develop a Plan B for when equipment problems arise

Now you're totally prepared to present. You know what to consider before you get to the site, what to look for once you're there, how best to set up, and how best to deliver your words and images. You've also learned techniques for the actual delivery:

- Things to do and to avoid while you're talking—microphone use, Plan B when things go wrong, having enough handouts
- How to evaluate your presentation, thank and solicit input from your audience, and learn from your mistakes

Now that you've mastered the effective use of technology when developing, planning, and making a presentation, uti-

lize Chapter 11 to learn more ways to use technology to benefit your speaking, training, or consulting business.

 Make a planning checklist for preparing for a presentation using the information in this chapter.

Arrive an extra half-hour earlier than usual at
your next presentation with the goal of preparing
the room early enough so that when people start to arrive,
you are free to greet them.

Best Practices

Technology planning, by definition, should be performed in advance of making decisions and taking actions. The following scenarios, checklists, and questions are designed to help you select the most appropriate tools for your technology toolkit and then use them to help you get the edge in using technology for your business.

Best practices represent guidelines and recommendations for making the most of your technology. When businesses of any size create technology plans, they define their needs, review their current capabilities, research best practices, and recommend changes that will enhance their ability to achieve their goals. Read through the following best practices for speakers, trainers, and consultants and see where they can help you with your use of technology.

FOCUS ON THE SOFTWARE YOU NEED

The biggest concern computer buyers have is obsolescence. "Can my system keep up with what's on the market?" It's a legitimate question, fueled by the daily barrage of newspaper, magazine, radio, and TV ads promoting the latest and greatest technology. The message of these ads causes you to question: can my computer do what my competitor's computer does? The answer to that question is maybe. You might have a newer, bigger, faster computer than the other person; you might not. It might not even matter. The better question to ask is whether your current system is capable of running the software that you need to serve your customers and advance your business. Here is how to zero in on the software you actually need.

Consider what jobs you need your computer to do. You can break this task down into three stages: the tangible output you need to deliver, the category of tools (in this case software) that will help you get the job done, and finally, the specific tools you need to accomplish your task.

Mike Rounds, a specialist in translating complicated technical ideas into human terms, reinforces this notion. He says, "Software gives you the power and flexibility—not the hardware. To be most effective, a computer should be the second item considered—after the software. Examine your actual and projected needs, locate software that will address those needs, and then select and acquire the computer hardware to run the software applications."

The tools listed in Table 11.1 are best-of-class, so you can't go wrong choosing from among those listed. Every one of these recommended software packages is available for both Windows and Macintosh systems.

BUDGET FOR UPDATES—PUSHING YOUR TECHEDGE COSTS MONEY AND TIME

The need for new hardware and software should come as no surprise. The average lifespan of a new computer is 3 to 5 years. Every 12 to 18 months, you will see upgrades to your business application and utility software.

Set aside 20 percent to 30 percent of the value of your hardware each year so you have replacement capital. Because software developers are constantly working on improving existing features and adding new capabilities, think of your software as an annual subscription rather than as a one-time investment. Budget 10 percent to 25 percent of your software

Table 11.1

Software Categories for Business Tasks

Outcome	Category	Software
Write proposals, speeches, articles, books, letters, marketing content	Word processing	ClarisWorks Microsoft Word
Manage contact information, mailing labels, reminders/to-do/tickler lists	Database management	FileMaker Pro ACT!
Create workbooks, job aids, marketing materials	Desktop publishing	Adobe PageMaker QuarkXPress
Slide show	Presentations	PowerPoint Astound!
Invoices, accounts receivable, accounts payable	Financial management	Intuit's Quicken
Connect to the Internet through a commercial online service	Communications software	America Online CompuServe MSN
Online research	Web browser	Netscape Navigator/Communicator Internet Explorer
Web site content	Web publishing	Adobe PageMill Claris Home Page Microsoft FrontPage
Inventory control	Database management	FileMaker Pro 4D

value annually for updates and upgrades. If you like to explore new software titles, you might want to set aside a discretionary budget line and stick to it to prevent yourself from going overboard.

To spread your technology dollars further:

■ Upgrade the RAM and hard drive capacity of your computers to extend their usable lifespan.

■ Your printer, monitor, keyboard, and other peripherals can be reused with new cpus. Be sure to factor in these savings.

■ If you need to bridge a gap between selling or donating (remember the tax write-off!) office equipment and the purchase of new equipment (remember the Christmas and post-show sales!), consider leasing. Companies that can help you in this area are listed on the web site **techedge.BillRingle.com**.

Make upgrades part of your business planning cycle and you will be able to project what hardware and software needs to be upgraded in a particular time frame. When you analyze the costs of your technology, be sure to factor in direct cost savings (such as long-distance phone and fax charges) and income enhancement (additional bookings, product sales, publicity).

DEVELOP AND FOLLOW
A BACKUP PLAN

Imagine that the next time you use your computer, it freezes on you. You try to restart and the start-up drive is not recognized. You attempt to start up from a troubleshooting disk and, even with the best recovery software, the hard drive will not mount on your desktop.

Welcome to the worst-case scenario; welcome to reality. Some computer technicians sarcastically note that there are only two types of computer users: those who have lost data and those who have not . . . yet. The point here is to take action now to prepare to deal with the worst-case scenario before it strikes.

A backup plan requires backup tools and a strategy for using the tools. For backing up sets of files, a Zip drive costs about $150 and each disk holds 100 MB. When you want to backup a large hard drive (greater than 1.2 MB), you will want to consider a tape drive, which also costs less than $200. All of these devices include software for scheduling backups on a regular basis.

Your back-up strategy might be to have weekly backups of all the data that has changed on your system. With multiple computers in your office, you will want to take advantage of the backup software to configure it to back up only documents that have changed. Avoid backing up applications (for which you have master disks) and your system folder (which can be restored from a CD or master disks). These files are not as critical as your document files—the presentations, client contacts, invoices, articles, books, research notes, and so on.

LEARN WHAT YOU OWN
BEFORE BUYING MORE

Investing in new software and hardware requires your involvement to yield dividends. Chris Clarke-Epstein, CSP, a self-described "technobabe," encourages her colleagues to resist the temptation to buy new software before thoroughly learning the software you already own.

Many computers come with software bundles loaded onto the hard drive at the time of purchase. This can be both an advantage and a disadvantage. On the positive side, you can acquire new software that you need because it helps you with your business. The downside of bundled software is that many useless games and low-quality clip art collections are added to inflate the list of titles included in the bundle.

 To increase your familiarity with the software you own:

- *Dedicate one hour a week to learning how new features of the program operate.*
- *Purchase a book on the topic (such as web page design) or program (such as FileMaker).*
- *Join a special interest group for this software at your local user group.*
- *Subscribe to a free Internet mailing list on the topic.*
- *Search the Internet for web sites highlighting this area.*

THE INTERNET SHORTENS THE DISTANCE BETWEEN YOU AND THE ANSWERS YOU NEED

One of the most significant and overlooked benefits of the resources available on the Internet is the savings they offer the average computer user in both money and time. You save money when you can get information online and do not have to buy new software; you save time when you can get the information in minutes rather than hours (after a trip to the local computer store) or the next day (when the software arrives via overnight courier).

Do you need to know a zip code? Ask the USPS web site (**www.usps.gov**). Want to check on the flight schedules going to a particular city? Give Travelocity a try (**www.travel ocity.com**). Looking to withdraw cash in a city away from home after a presentation? Find the closest ATM machine (**visa.infonow.net/powersearch.html**). How about a good movie? Complete listings are a few clicks away on your laptop computer (**www.movielink.com**). Would you quote the title of the pending legislation in your presentation to show the group you are aware of issues important to its industry if you could double-check your facts easily? Easy! For Senate legislation check **www.senate.gov**, or for House of Representatives information check www.house.gov. Visit the TechEdge web site (**techedge.BillRingle.com**) when you want more up-to-date tips.

LABEL YOUR CABLES

Finding information on the Internet is not very hard once you learn your way around, and setting up your computer cables is even easier. If you have a single desktop system with a power cord, keyboard, mouse, monitor, modem, and printer, then this is a trivial task. The cable connectors fit into industry-standard sockets on the back of the computer. On many systems, icons label the purpose of each socket. For instance, you might see a picture of a printer above the printer port. These icons are designed to give you additional cues about which cables belong in what sockets.

The picture becomes a bit more complex when you travel with a computer and projection device. Now you have video-out cables with multiple ends for different projection device inputs. You have cables from the LCD panel or projector. You may have additional audio input and audio amplifier cables to keep straight. Even though you did it comfortably on your kitchen table before you left for the presentation, it's suddenly a different story when you are on stage with 20 minutes to go before your talk begins!

TECH TIP *When you travel with technology, be sure to label your cables. The primary reason to do this is to make your life easier during set-up. Use labels that wrap around the cable itself and write a note of where this cable goes and what it is used for—whatever will help jog your memory. A simple* *wiring diagram is also a good idea but is not a substitute for well-labled cables. A second reason to label cables is to be sure you can claim them when you pack up and leave. An easy way to identify your cables is to fold a business card over the cable and staple the loose ends together close enough to prevent it from sliding off.*

REMEMBER LOW TECH

In the rush to get on the information superhighway and other techno-bandwagons, remember the seemingly low-tech aides to delivering a good presentation and running your business.

■ Always have plenty of water nearby as you speak; sipping fluids helps your voice stay strong. Avoid ice water because the temperature can chill your vocal cords, which constricts your throat.
■ Fill out registration and warranty cards for the equipment you buy. Companies will mail you upgrade notices and perhaps offer special discounts on hardware and software.
■ An electric typewriter (with correction ribbon!) can save you hours of aggravation in filling in forms and envelopes.

When speakers, trainers, or consultants think of developing their skills, whether it is their tech edge or any other growing edge, they often look at the most advanced (and often the most costly) technology. Remember that the edge you are developing is your own, and it is different for each individual. A low-tech approach is a way of being thrifty and innovative, but it is not easy for some people, especially "early adopters."

People who learn about and use cutting-edge technologies as soon as they are available are called early adopters. Early adopters usually spend a lot of time fiddling with gadgets and pay a premium to do so. You know you are an early adopter if you were one of the first to own a fax machine, home computer, cellular phone, or personal digital assistant (PDA) or to have tested prerelease beta software. It's exciting to learn about these new technologies. It is also expensive in terms of time and dollars.

Taking the high-tech road is not easy for an early adopter for three reasons: (1) You have no choice—the fascination with techology is an inherent part of your nature. (2) High tech at its outset is more costly. Over time, the price premium is reduced as the installed base increases. (3) High tech is often misunderstood and unappreciated by non-early adopters.

The part of me that is an early adopter can be traced back more than 25 years to when I learned Morse code to pass my amateur (ham) radio test and built robots for school science fairs. As a professional early adopter, I learned good computing practices the hard way, having to reconstruct hard drives after testing software for companies, such as Microsoft, Claris, and Symantec, that you would expect to "know better than to make such a mistake." To paraphrase futurist Joel Barker, "You can always tell the pioneers by the arrows in their backs." Early adopters may also find that their enthusiasm for a new product or technology is not widely shared. I wrote and delivered training courses on using the Internet for business when most people thought a web site was something the janitor eliminated with a broom.

While everyone can benefit from remembering the low-tech approach to using technology, early adopters will benefit most from doing so. It is simply a matter of swapping your technologist hat for your business hat in order to make a decision or gain an insight. As an early adopter, it's great to have the hottest new technology toys. As a businessperson, you want to invest your time and money where they will lead to the greatest returns in service capabilities, product quality, and administrative functioning.

For example, buying the latest computer with all the whizzy features might feel important at the moment. However, if you really examined what you needed to use the computer for, you might realize you could save 40 percent or more by purchasing a model that came out 12 months ago that dealers need to unload to make more space for the newer models arriving. You won't be on this year's "cutting edge," but you will have hundreds of dollars more in your bank account that you can devote to other projects.

High tech is not always the way to go for practical reasons. Voice-to-text technology, for example, has been around since the early 1990s. However, you would be better off dictating into a hand-held tape recorder and having it transcribed later than using your notebook computer's voice-to-text capability just because it's high tech.

THINK BEYOND YOUR DESKTOP/NOTEBOOK COMPUTER

A cartoon shows Dilbert sitting in front of his home computer. His girlfriend complains, "You love that computer more than me, don't you?!" Dilbert turns his head over his shoulder to say to her, "No, I don't," and then turns back to his computer. In the third panel, he nervously hopes to himself, "Please don't ask about my laptop!" Evidently, the answer to that question from his girlfriend would be more complicated.

One reason Dilbert's view was so narrow is that he didn't have the benefit of TechEdge! Here are some points to stimulate your thinking in this area:

- Consider how palmtop computers might serve your needs. The *Wall Street Journal* called the Pilot 2000 the "high tech toy of the year." Being able to carry a contact list, calendar, directions, and notes around in a small, lightweight package could have its advantages if you travel or attend meetings a great deal. Be sure your palmtop computer has the capability to synchronize data with your laptop to avoid the most awkward aspect of palmtops: the tiny keyboards and/or writing stylus.

- Consider online connectivity to be a high-priority reason for owning your computer. The Internet is an amazing resource. It can be considered the biggest shared hard drive the world has ever known. Every day you can find more value—new databases, information pages, support sites, quotes, requests for speaking engagements, and more. Just remember that it takes skill and practice to master.

- Before the year 2000, you will find more and more non-computer devices connected to the Internet due to the ease of access this networking platform offers. It is technically easy to connect gas pumps, vending machines, bowling lanes, parking lot spots, and even movie theater seats to networks for private or public access. Savvy speakers, consultants, and trainers will be on the lookout for this trend and will help shape the new ways technology assists us to learn, do business, and otherwise interact on many levels in our society.

By looking at systems below your desktop (portable palmtops) as well as systems beyond it (the resource-rich Internet), you will maintain a better perspective on the capabilities and usefulness of your office technology.

E-MAIL IS A CRITICAL BUSINESS TOOL

For the modest investment of the few hours needed to learn how to use it and about $20 per month (once you have your computer and modem, that is), e-mail is one of the best ways to contact people and exchange information. No other means of communications offers you the speed, reliability, and flexibility of e-mail. While not everyone in the country has access to e-mail, the majority of the people with whom you do business now or with whom you would like to do business in the future have e-mail and are using it more effectively each year.

Here are a few additional tips on how to grow your TechEdge with e-mail.

Remember the Portability of E-Mail

Regardless of whether your e-mail account is with a commercial online service or an ISP, you can access it from anywhere on the Internet as easily as you retrieve phone messages from any telephone with a dial tone. International airports such as Heathrow (London) and Nakita (Tokyo) offer direct high-speed connections for the wired traveler; in the United States, Internet kiosks are becoming more common, allowing users to check mail or browse the web. AOL provides hundreds of local area dial-up points from around the world and a premium-charge 800 number for locales not yet served by local numbers. If your e-mail is served from an ISP, you can read that e-mail from any Internet connection, such as on a corporate, university, or conference center network.

Think Before You Send

Access to e-mail is ubiquitous. Common sense and common courtesy in e-mail messages is not, unfortunately. Like any powerful tool, it can be dangerous if used carelessly. Remember that e-mail can be sent or forwarded to any number of people with the click of a mouse, intentionally or accidentally. You do not want to find yourself in the position of the

New York advertising agency vice president who inadvertently sent the company's salary and bonus list to the entire company rather than just to the human resources director.

Simplify Contact Information

In an attempt to appear accessible online, businesspeople sometimes list e-mail addresses on their business cards and other collateral material. This is a well-intentioned idea that can backfire quickly. Your goal is not to show people how many online services you subscribe to (one for AOL, one for CompuServe, one for your local ISP, . . .), but rather to indicate the address at which you prefer to be contacted. Listing several e-mail addresses is a carry-over from the bad old days when e-mail gateways did not allow mail to travel between different systems easily. That has all changed, and any system that you are likely to use for e-mail will be able to send and receive messages from any other Internet system.

I can relate to having several e-mail accounts due to the different system administration roles that I perform. At any given time, I can have a dozen or more active e-mail accounts. It would drive me crazy to have to check each one several times a day whether I am in the office or on the road. Instead, I follow two simple guidelines: (1) I give all my e-mail accounts on any e-mail system the same name whenever possible, and (2) I forward all secondary e-mail to my primary StarComm account, which I check throughout the day when I'm in the office and at least twice a day when I'm presenting seminars or delivering keynotes for out-of-town clients.

Pick one e-mail address and stick with it. If you can, forward your mail from the other accounts to your primary e-mail address. It will clarify the path for your customers and colleagues to reach you and save you the time and trouble of checking several e-mail accounts on a regular basis.

Subscribe to Internet Mailing Lists

Internet mailing lists offer a way to expand your contacts, meet new people with similar interests, solve problems, and build communities online. Best of all, many of them do not charge a membership fee.

Subscribing or unsubscribing to an Internet mailing list is as easy as sending an e-mail message to the list administrator address with three items in the body of the message: the word *subscribe* or *unsubscribe,* the name of the list, and your full name. It's a powerful, simple way to maximize your use of e-mail.

Be careful not to join too many lists, and be careful of lists that have unusual rules or restrictions. Monitor how much mail you are getting via Internet mail lists. With Internet mailing lists, it is easy to overdo a good thing. The best discussion mailing lists practice two policies: (1) They keep their function clear. Announcement newsletters are one-way, edited, brief updates on timely products and services. Discussion lists are collaborative efforts of the group, which can be sent to members as summary digests, if desired. The success of any online communications vehicle can be measured in its "signal-to-noise" ratio: how much valuable content versus fluff advertising, promotion, or poor-quality content is present. (2) If a list's purpose is support, then two forms of message predominate: questions for help and summaries of the help the requester received. Good lists have active participants who share an understanding of what types of communications to expect and do not stray far from that purpose.

CUSTOMIZATION IS THE KEY TO SUCCESS

As you advance in your experience and reputation as a speaker, trainer, and/or consultant, you will come to recognize the importance of customization. In this instance, customization refers to two areas: the materials you present for clients and the materials you use to market your business.

With your clients, research their organizations so you can customize

- slides
- workbooks
- presentation examples

Definitely include the names of key officers of the company, especially those who will be in attendance at your presentation. But go beyond that level of customization to stand out. Understand the most urgent and important issues the organization is facing and adapt your talk to address them. Request the company's annual report, newsletter, marketing materials, and other relevant documents to study in advance. Visit its web site. Interview managers and staff via phone and e-mail. Incorporate what you learn into your presentation and training materials. Avoid being one of those "professionals" who takes out a cue card at the beginning of the talk that prompts them to say "Hey, it's great to be here in <insert name of city> with you folks from <insert name of company>. . . ." and call that customization.

Marketing your business involves creating a distinct appearance on paper and online that is congruent with your mission as well as your style. At every opportunity to make a design decision, consider whether using a standard template adds to or detracts from your professional image. Think about this when choosing the background pattern for your professional portraits, for your PowerPoint slide presentations, and for all your printed materials from your workbooks down to your business cards.

HIRE THE HELP YOU NEED

Remember the value of partnerships in business. When tackling a significant project, it helps to have the advice of someone who has explored this territory ahead of you and developed skills in this area. Wherever your growing edge happens to be, someone else is probably able to shed some light on the problems you are facing, from buying a computer system to cracking into a new market, to self-publishing a book, to developing your web site.

My recommendation in this area differs from presenters who say to an audience, "Ask your friends what they use and then do the same." That advice is more comforting than useful. Your friend or associate may not have the same current needs as you do and may not need the same capabilities you do.

A trainer friend of mine was advised by her staff person to purchase new computer equipment because it would lead to tens of thousands of dollars worth of new product sales, provide more choices in software, and create an easier work environment. Spending $10,000 in new hardware and software didn't seem like such a risk, given the promised payoff. However, after spending thousands of dollars for equipment, the staff person learned what she needed to in order to get a new job somewhere else and left. The trainer's business was stuck with the new equipment, which works fine, but with no one trained to use it—a disastrous expense. Book and tape sales would have been better served by investing the money in marketing to increase the target market's awareness of the company's resources. A good computer business consultant would have provided an objective analysis, taking into account the experience and expectations of the staff, the goals of the business owner, and resources available to accomplish those goals.

It is not enough that a prospective consultant or advisor says that he or she "knows a lot about this subject." It is your money you are spending to improve your business. You will want to get a return on your investment of time and money. Here are several guidelines for hiring experts/partners/consultants:

- Look for real-world experience that has produced tangible results for others. Find out if the prospect performed similar work for other clients or in a previous position. Make sure you are not hiring someone who is simply "a chapter ahead" of you and your staff.
- Ask for references and follow them up. Ask the references to describe the work performed, whether it was done on time and within budget, and whether they would hire the person/firm again. If you speak to at least three references, a pattern will emerge that will help you understand whether you will be satisfied with this consultant. If you have trouble reaching the references, ask for more from the consultant.
- Educational background is important in technology and business consulting. Formal study indicates a deep background and commitment to the subject area. Certification is also important. Graphic artists who attended a series of courses to learn to produce graphics for the web are better equipped to work on a large project for our company than are ones who learn on the job. Both degrees and certifications show that an individual was willing to invest in his or her own education and training.
- Quality generally costs more, but it is not always the most expensive option. This applies to consultant's fees, computer equipment, and many other areas of business. Get written competitive bids from a variety of sources to understand the playing field. One very costly approach is to dabble in areas that are not your core business. For instance, I know a business owner who has converted her contact database to a new system several times in the past

three years becuase "it seemed like a good idea." She wasted dollars and hours on projects that did not produce better results or improved business functionality in the end. Selecting a developer from among several bids to create a single system that met her business needs might have cost more than a do-it-yourself solution, but it would have allowed her to focus on delivering services or developing products that would have covered the cost of the project.

■ Once you have someone who produces quality results, communicates well with you and your staff, and improves his or her own skills, build a long-term relationship with him or her.

JOIN A USER GROUP
AND MAKE FRIENDS

One of the best places to learn about computer technology is a user group. Find the closest user group meeting and attend a session. In addition to becoming familiar with new computer solutions, you will also meet many interesting and talented people who can serve as consultants and trainers for your business. It is best to meet these people in a casual setting to develop relationships with them before you have an urgent need. As business owner, speaker, and author Harvey Mackay says, "Dig your well *before* you're thirsty."

LEADERS ARE READERS

Using technology in your business requires a certain level of familiarity with the tools, techniques, and jargon. Face-to-face contact is often the best way to learn for some people. For others, reading is the best approach. In either case, you can develop your skills and understanding by spending time each month reading a few articles from a computer magazine.

Some presenters recoil at the thought. Responses range from, "They're too technical," to, "I've never seen anything I could use in one of those magazines." Fear not—publishers have produced a wide range of magazines to appeal to different levels of interest, background, and experience. Good beginning magazines include *Home Office Computing* and *Family PC. Internet User* and *Yahoo! Internet Life* are interesting reads for Internet-specific content.

A low-pressure way to find out if these magazines are right for you is to visit a local Borders Bookstore or Barnes & Noble, where they have terrific magazine displays and in-store cafes. Pick up a couple of the magazines, order a drink and a muffin, and peruse the magazines. After reading a few articles, you will know whether it contains information that is appropriate for your needs and interests. Lastly, remember your online sources of information. Bookmark sites mentioned in TechEdge as well as those you find on your own.

WEB SITES ARE JUST THE FIRST STEP

Visiting web sites gives you access to information and resources. Surfing the web can provide hours of entertainment and learning, but to find answers.

Providing information to others about your business via a web site extends your reach. It is important to constantly market your web site to increase online awareness, updating the material so that people find value in returning to the site time after time, and referring to the web site address in your printed materials.

The more you can individualize the sites you visit frequently, the better. Chapter 5 explains how to create a webliography. Create webliographies for discovering in-depth information about your industry, your competition, as well as sites that you find entertaining.

PRESENTING: RESPONSIBILITIES AND REWARDS

Preparation is the key to successful high-tech presentations. Chapter 10 lists the best practices for planning, rehearsing, and testing your presentations. Remember to use a high-capacity storage device like a Zip drive to hold all the software, fonts, and copies of your presentations.

USE YOUR COMPUTER TO MAKE YOUR LIFE EASIER AND YOUR BUSINESS STRONGER

Technology makes a terrific servant but a terrible master. Be clear about the tasks that you wish to accomplish and then ask yourself how your tools can help you achieve this objective. Remember to select from the entire range of low-tech and high-tech tools, because the best tool for the job is the one that helps you get the job done faster, better, and less expensively than without it. Set goals to advance your own technology edge, and learn more each day. Your confidence will grow and so will your business.

SUMMARY

The concept of "best practices" can be thought of as a philosophy of applying well-thought-out professional and technical methods to aid and protect your business concerns. In Chapter 16, you've learned to apply time-honored methods used by professionals in diverse fields to the business needs of a speaker, trainer, or consultant:

- Choosing and updating software
- Backing up vital data and applications on your computer
- Deciding when to buy new hardware or software
- Leveraging the Internet's resources to reduce costs

- Setting up your computer equipment, both in the office and on the road
- Deciding when to go high-tech or low-tech
- Maintaining your perspective on technology
- Making best use of e-mail
- Customizing presentations for your clientele
- Finding employees, consultants, and outside services
- Networking (in the personal sense) with other technology users through user groups
- Keeping current by reading professional journals
- Utilizing the World Wide Web, not just browsing it
- Presenting responsibly
- Making your computer work for you (not the other way around!)

Remember these tips and maintain your TechEdge!

 Visit the web site of a major backup hardware or software manufacturer, such as Iomega (**www. iomega.com**), McAfee (**www.mcafee.com**), or Symantec (**www.symantec.com**), and look for further information on backup strategies for your computer's data and applications.

About Toastmasters International

If the thought of public speaking is enough to stop you dead in your tracks, it may have the same effect on your career.

While surveys report that public speaking is one of people's most dreaded fears, the fact remains that the inability to effectively deliver a clear thought in front of others can spell doom for professional progress. The person with strong communication skills has a clear advantage over tongue-tied colleagues—especially in a competitive job market.

Toastmasters International, a nonprofit educational organization, helps people conquer their pre-speech jitters. From one club started in Santa Ana, California, in 1924, the organization now has more than 170,000 members in 8,300 clubs in 62 countries.

How Does It Work?

A Toastmasters club is a "learn by doing" workshop in which men and women hone their communication and leadership skills in a friendly, supportive atmosphere. A typical club has 20 members who meet weekly or biweekly to practice public speaking techniques. Members, who pay approximately $35 in dues twice a year, learn by progressing through a series of 10 speaking assignments and being evaluated on their performance by their fellow club members. When finished with the basic speech manual, members can select from among 14 advanced programs that are geared toward specific career needs. Members also have the opportunity to develop and practice leadership skills by working in the High Performance Leadership Program.

Besides taking turns to deliver prepared speeches and evaluate those of other members, Toastmasters give impromptu talks on assigned topics, usually related to current events. They also develop listening skills, conduct meetings, learn parliamentary procedure and gain leadership experience by serving as club officers. But most importantly, they develop self-confidence from accomplishing what many once thought impossible.

The benefits of Toastmasters' proven and simple learning formula has not been lost on the thousands of corporations that sponsor in-house Toastmasters clubs as cost-efficient means of satisfying their employees' needs for communication training. Toastmasters clubs can be found in the U.S. Senate and the House of Representatives, as well as in a variety of community organizations, prisons, universities, hospitals, military bases, and churches.

How to Get Started

Most cities in North America have several Toastmasters clubs that meet at different times and locations during the week. If you are interested in forming or joining a club, call (714) 858-8255. For a listing of local clubs, call (800) WE-SPEAK, or write Toastmasters International, PO Box 9052, Mission Viejo, California 92690, USA. You can also visit our website at http://www.toastmasters.org.

As the leading organization devoted to teaching public speaking skills, we are devoted to helping you become more effective in your career and daily life.

Terrence J. McCann
Executive Director, Toastmasters International

About the National Speaker's Association

The National Speakers Association (NSA) is an international association of more than 3,700 members dedicated to advancing the art and value of experts who speak professionally. Specific purposes of NSA are:

- Defining and supporting standards of excellence in professional speaking;
- Enhancing the communication competencies and business skills of professional speakers;
- Promoting the value of professional speakers as effective sources of expertise, knowledge and insight; and
- Expanding the marketplace for professional speaking.

NSA delivers a multifaceted environment for advancing the careers of professional speakers. Virtually all of NSA's programs, meetings, publications and resources are structured around eight professional competencies. Together, they are designed to give organization and substance to the educational and professional advancement of each member. The professional competencies are: Authorship and Product Development; Managing the Business; Platform Mechanics; Presenting and Performing; Professional Awareness; Professional Relationships; Sales and Marketing; and Topic Development.

The programming for NSA's Educational Workshops, Annual Conventions and single-focus Learning Labs are based on these competencies. While a minimum number of paid presentations must be documented to qualify a speaker for membership in NSA, nonmembers are welcome to attend chapter and national meetings and can subscribe to *Professional Speaker* magazine.

For more information, contact the National Speakers Association, 1500 S. Priest Drive, Tempe, Arizona 85281; Phone: 602-968-2552; Fax: 602-968-0911; E-mail: nsamain@aol.com; Web Site: http://www.nsa speaker.org.